Questioning Empowerment

Working with Women in Honduras

Jo Rowlands

Oxfam
(UK and Ireland)

Quaker author

cover photograph: Mike Goldwater/Oxfam

Available from the following agents:
for Canada and the USA: Humanities Press International, 165 First Avenue, Atlantic Highlands, New Jersey NJ 07716-1289, USA; tel. (908) 8721441; fax (908) 8720717
for Southern Africa: David Philip Publishers, PO Box 23408, Claremont, Cape Town 7735, South Africa; tel. (021) 644136; fax (021) 643358

Available in Ireland from Oxfam in Ireland, 19 Clanwilliam Terrace, Dublin 2. Tel: 01 661 8544

Published by Oxfam (UK and Ireland) 274 Banbury Road, Oxford OX2 7DZ

OX412/RB/97

Printed by Oxfam Print Unit

Oxfam UK and Ireland is a registered charity no. 202918, and is a member of Oxfam International.

Contents

Preface

My own interest in 'empowerment' dates from my experiences first as a community and peace activist and then as a feminist in the late 1970s. I was involved in many discussions about power, the forms it can take, the way one achieves/obtains/creates/wields it and so on, particularly in the context of non-violent direct action campaigning.[1] The issue of how to translate principles into practice was a very live one, and we talked about 'empowerment' as part of processes of social change. That preoccupation continued into my feminist activism, where along with others, I developed an analysis of oppression, first around gender and then class, race, disability, age and sexual orientation. Issues of power — who has it, who does not — continued to interest me in my work as a management consultant with non-government organisations.

So when I started to work with 'Third World' organisations and I immersed myself in the development and gender-and-development literature, I was both pleased and irritated, as well as interested, to find 'empowerment' being used as a concept, particularly in relation to women. Pleased, because it fitted with my own conceptions of what is important in the work for equality, liberation, and justice; and irritated because of the lack of exactitude. Issues of power seem to me utterly fundamental to the debate, yet they are so rarely explicitly addressed. I found myself agreeing with Sarah White that 'it is in its avoidance of discussing power that the fundamental weakness of the literature on women and development lies'.[2]

When I came across 'the empowerment approach' to gender planning I realised that I wanted to take a closer look at the meaning of empowerment in a development setting, and specifically, at empowerment in the context of women's organisations: what it is, and how it can be encouraged, especially in the light of Kabeer's conclusion that:

If there is a single most important lesson for feminists to learn from the past decades of development, it is that the political will for taking on more politically controversial issues which address women's strategic gender interests is contingent on women themselves organising to demand and promote change.[3]

Development is, after all, about change. Does empowerment imply any specific kinds of changes, and if so, for whom? In this book, I give an account of the ground I have covered so far in exploring empowerment. My thanks are due to the British Economic and Social Research Council for the financial support they gave me in my research. It was not my intention, however, to produce a piece of academic research in the somehow-unconnected-to-real-life sense that is often read into that word. Rather, I wanted to undertake a theoretically and intellectually grounded exploration of the concept that would enable an analysis of the practical and organisational implications of its use. I did not undertake this from some supposedly 'neutral' standpoint, but from the position of an individual committed to the achievement of justice and liberation, for women and for other people who share that struggle.

I have focused this work specifically on women's empowerment, but I believe the account holds much of relevance to the empowerment of other disadvantaged groups. I would encourage readers whose primary concern is not women or gender issues to 'read between the lines' in order to consider what of my account may be applicable to other contexts.

In this book I set out to provide a definition for the term 'empowerment', looking in particular at how it might be used in relation to women, using a gender and development analysis. My intention is to encourage more precise usage and to explore how a more disciplined use of the concept of empowerment might provide a useful tool for activism, gender planning, project planning, and evaluation.

Structure of the book

'Empowerment' is a concept used by people who hold a wide range of views, to the right and left of the political spectrum. How is it that such a diverse range of people can talk of 'empowerment' with enthusiasm? How has 'empowerment' come to 'fit' with the various ideologies; can they mean the same by it? If, as I suspect, they do not, does 'empowerment' have meanings that are useful in the gender-development debate and in the practice that arises from it? What are the implications of empowerment for activists, development agencies, and other professionals?

These are some of the questions that I had in my mind when I embarked on the work that led to this book. The first of those questions is touched on briefly in chapter 1. The second is the subject of chapter 2; and the third and fourth, the rest of the book. Much of the existing literature on empowerment as it relates to gender and development originates from or uses examples in South Asia. In contrast, my work here uses case-study material from Honduras in Central America.

Any discussion of empowerment needs a context. In chapter 1, I examine the way in which the concept of empowerment within development thinking is part of shifting emphases within the development 'discourse' — the collection of ideas, concepts, images and words with which development is portrayed. I also explore various uses of the concept within the theoretical framework of women, gender, and development. These necessarily brief accounts show clearly that 'empowerment' has not arisen in a vacuum, but forms part of attempts to resolve some of the difficulties which arise from discrepancies between theoretical approaches, practical approaches, and the needs and aspirations of real people in difficult circumstances.

Chapter 2 charts my exploration of the concept of empowerment. I take a detour into the various definitions of power offered within the literature in English of the social sciences, and from that base, consider the meaning of empowerment within a development context and the ways it has been used by different writers, as a background for the case studies which follow.

Chapter 3 provides what is intended to be just enough background information about Honduras to enable the reader unfamiliar with the country or the region to picture the lives and conditions of the women and the organisations I describe in the following two chapters. The first of these organisations, the subject of chapter 4, is a Health Promoters' training programme in Urraco Pueblo; the second, in chapter 5, is the *Programa Educativo de la Mujer* (PAEM, Women's Educational Programme). For each case study there is a specific contextual account and a description of the activities, structures, and achievements of the women and the organisation concerned. That is followed by an analysis of the various elements which contributed to (or impeded) those achievements. The cases are presented in considerable detail in order to enable the reader to reach their own view. From this, in Chapter Six, I move on to explore the commonalities and differences between the two organisations in order to propose a picture of empowerment which can provide a model on which to draw in considering other cases or future activities.

Finally, in chapter 7, I consider the implications of empowerment, using the model I have developed here, for activists and grassroots organisations, for development agencies, and for professionals working in development. There are implications for the continuing theoretical discussion of empowerment, as process, as a gender issue, and as a development issue. There are significant methodological implications; there are implications for organisational structure. There are also implications for the role of the 'change agent' and the supporting organisation. Empowerment, therefore, is not a term to use lightly and without careful consideration.

This book is a shortened and edited version of my PhD thesis: 'Empowerment examined: an exploration of the concept and practice of women's empowerment in Honduras', 1995, University of Durham.

A glossary of Spanish terms used in the text and a list of abbreviations can be found on pages (ref); the exhaustive bibliography developed for the thesis is given in full on page .

A note on methodology

The case studies in this volume derive from research undertaken in 1991-5. Between November 1992 and September 1993 I interviewed women in two women's organisations in northern Honduras, generating over 70 hours of individual interviews with group members and group discussions. Anyone interested in the specifics of the methodology used, both in generating the material and in its analysis, can find a detailed account in Rowlands (1995). It is perhaps also worth stating the obvious here: that both organisations will have moved on from the snapshots I provide, and changes will have happened since I undertook the interviews.

Acknowledgements

A book like this does not materialise without the input, direct or indirect, of many people. I would like to thank everyone who contributed to my research and the process of turning it into a thesis and now a book. In particular, because they contributed well beyond any call of duty or friendship, I would like to mention Janet Townsend, Ruth Ingram, and Deborah Eade. And, of course, all the women and men in Honduras who co-operated so openly and generously.

Jo Rowlands
April 1997

List of abbreviations

ACPH Asociación Cultural Popular Hondureña
(Honduran Association for Popular Culture)

ADP Asociación para el Desarollo Popular
(Association for Popular Development

AFL American Federation of Labour

AHDEJUMUR Honduran Association
for the Development of Youth and Women

AIDS Acquired Immuno Deficency Syndrome

ANACH Asociación Nacional de Campesinos Hondureños
(National Association of Honduran Peasants

ANAMUC Asociación Nacional de Mujeres Campesinas
(National Association of Peasant Women)

ANDAR (Andar = to walk)

ASEPADE Asesores para el Desarollo (Consultants for Development)

CAFOD Catholic Fund for Overseas Development

CARITAS (Catholic charitable organisation)

CCD Comisión Cristiano par el Desarollo
(Christian Commission for Development)

CDM Centro para los Derechos de la Mujer
(Centre for Women's Rights) (formerly CLADEM-H)

CEM Centro de Estudios de la Mujer (Centre for Women's Studies)

CNTC National Union of Rural Workers

CODEMUH Colectivo de Mujeres Hondureñas
(Collective of Honduran Women)

CODIMCA Consejo para el Desarollo Integrado de la Mujer Campesina
(Council for the Integrated Development of Peasant Women)

COMUNICA (NGO working with NGOs
and Popular Organisations on Communication)

DAWN Development Alternatives with Women for a New Era

FEHMUC Honduran Federation of Peasant Women

FFHC/AD Freedom from Hunger Campaign/Action for Development

GAD Gender and Development

GEM Grupo para la Educación Popular de Mujeres
(Popular Education Group for Women, Mexico)

FENACH Federación Nacional de Campesinos Hondureños
(National Federation of Honduran Peasants)

FHIS Fondo Hondureño de Inversión Social
(Honduran Fund for Social Investment)

FUTH Federación Unitaria de Trabajadores de Honduras
(United Federation of Workers)

GDP Gross Domestic Product

GNP Gross National Product

HIV Human Immuno-deficiency Virus

IHMA Instituto Hondureño de Mercadeo Agricula
(Honduran Institute for Agricultural Marketing)

INA Instituto Nacional Agrario (National Agrarian Institute)

MOMUCLAA Movimiento de Mujeres de la Colónia Lopez Arellano y
Area (Women's Movement of Colonia Lopez Arellano and Area)

NGDO Non-Government Development Organisation

NGO Non-Government Organisation

OCH Organisación Campesino Hondureño
(Organisation of Honduran Peasants)

ODA Overseas Development Administration

OPD Organismo Privado de Desarollo
(Private Development Organisation)

ORIT Organización Regional Interamericana del Trabajado
(Inter-American Regional Organisation of Labour)

PAEM Programa Educativo de la Mujer
(Women's Educational Programme)

PCH Partido Comunista de Honduras (Honduran Communist Party)

PDCH Partido Demócrata Cristiano Hondureño
(Honduran Christian Democrat Party)

PINU Partido de Innovación y Unidad (Innovation and Unity Party)

PL Partido Liberal (Liberal Party)

PN Partido Nacional (National Party)

SECPLAN Secretaría de Planificación, Coordinación y Presupuesto
(Secretariat of Planning, Co-ordination and Budget)

SEWA Self-Employed Women's Association (India)

SITRATERCO Sindicato de Trabajadores de la Tela Railroad Company
(Union of Workers for the Tela Railroad Company)

SNV (Dutch development agency)

UN United Nations

UNC Unión Nacional Campesino (National Peasant Union)

UNDP United Nations Development Programme

UNICEF United Nations Children's Fund

UNISA Unidad de Servicios para Fomentar la Participación
de la Mujer Hondureña (Services Unit for encouraging the
participation of Honduran Women)

USAID United States Agency for International Development

WAD Women and Development

WID Women in Development

1

Introduction

What is this word 'empowerment'? It is used frequently, and is no longer a word used only by the unconventional or fringe activist; it has become an acceptable, even, perhaps, a necessary part of the vocabulary of the mainstream development thinker or policy maker. Two examples show this clearly:

*Many basic services ... are best managed at the local level — even the village level — with the central agencies providing only technical advice and specialist inputs. The aims should be **to empower ordinary people** to take charge of their lives, to make communities more responsible for their development, and to make governments listen to their people. Fostering a more pluralistic structure — including non-governmental organisations ... — is a means to these ends.*
(World Bank, 1989)[1]

*Participation means that people are closely involved in the economic, social, cultural and political processes that affect their lives. Since participation requires increased influence and control, it also demands **increased empowerment** — in economic, social and political terms.* (UNDP, 1993)[2]

Does this usage of the word reflect the possible meanings of 'empowerment' that emerge from interviews with women in rural Honduras and from learning materials they use, or is the official view something entirely different? First, Teresa, Margarita, and Esperanza (here, and elsewhere, the names have been changed, for reasons of confidentiality):

... we knew what was happening to us and that we had to find our own solutions. People from outside couldn't do that for us... they would only know what we had told them about things, but the people who knew about our problems were us.
(Teresa, 50-year-old grandmother, 'animator' of women's group)

1

When I started I was embarrassed even with the other women. We met, talked a bit; you begin to talk in meetings, have more confidence. Then later, in the domestic work in the home, the way you behave... You change a lot with your husband and children. You learn things there that you didn't know. It helps a lot... When you start you're shy; now ... I rarely feel shy, because of what I've learned. (Margarita, 36-year-old group member)

I have [confidence] with whoever; ... now I will not be shy, but before I would stay like that to one side of the door. 'Come in' , 'oh no'; or 'come and eat', 'no I'm not hungry'; I was so shy. Today, no. If there's food you have to eat. So that's how things have been, I've woken up, and I know things.
(Esperanza, 47-year-old grandmother, 'animator' of women's group)

These words are echoed in words published by peasant women for peasant women (see also page 107):

Many of us have got used to having sad, negative thoughts. And sometimes we don't even want to think. But if we cultivate our minds with love, if we apply fertilizer, if we keep pulling up the weeds which unsettle us and sowing good quality seeds, little by little we will discover, with happiness, that our minds produce new, beautiful fruits. Fear and shame will begin to disappear, if we have the courage to overcome them and encourage ourselves to learn and to think new, unknown things. (PAEM, 1990).

We have seen that many of us have the same problems. For example, in our village there is no water, no light, no adequate school, no land to work, no employment, no health centre or medicines or nurses and food is scarcer and more expensive every day. All this is an injustice that makes us feel bad. But if because of this situation we keep complaining and spending time in talk, making ourselves victims, we are like the cat which chases its own tail. We go round in circles and do nothing.

But if we see these injustices and feel angry, that's good, so long as we do not take it out on our children. This anger should make us look for possible solutions. Because most other women in the country have the problems we have. We need to stop being individualistic; we need to join with other women who have the same problems and interests. We need to learn to unite, getting to know ourselves, regaining our dignity and identity, actively participating in our group, in our community, in our country. With faith, hope and happiness, because we are constructing a new form of living. (PAEM, 1990)

It is clear that 'empowerment' is used in many ways and in a wide range of contexts. Within the context of 'Third World'[3] development, the word appears in the language of, among others, neo-liberals, neo-Marxists, feminists, and Third World grassroots groups.[4] It will be useful to start with an understanding of the way the notion of empowerment fits into the theoretical frameworks most commonly used. I will therefore give a brief account of how empowerment can be related to development theory. That will be followed by an account of the theory on women and gender in a development context. This will provide an important background for the chapters which follow, since empowerment, as part of development thinking, while by no means of exclusive relevance to women and gender issues, has been predominantly discussed in that context. However, as Chapter Two will show, empowerment has also been used in relation to race, disability and other aspects of social identity; and the focus of this book on women and gender need not prevent the ideas being applied elsewhere.

Development theory

Within the political right, the dominant ideology of neo-liberalism and a monetarist approach to economics have held sway throughout the 1980s and early 1990s in many countries of the world, promoted and supported by the major international financial institutions. There has been a loss of faith in the state as the automatic prime mover of development processes, and an increasing emphasis, in neo-liberal economic theory, on private bodies, both commercial companies and non-state organisations. It became evident, however, in the latter half of the 1980s and the early 1990s, that undiluted neo-liberal policies were not preventing the escalation of the Third World debt crisis and were having unacceptable consequences in particular for the poorest and most vulnerable. Ideas of 'development with a human face' began to emerge,[5] along with attempts to incorporate non-economic issues into the development agenda, for example, in the UNDP's *Human Development Index,* published in 1993. Although this 'humanising' approach brought a fresh emphasis on the role of the state in development, there was growing interest in non-governmental organisations (NGOs) as development agents, in activity at the grassroots, and in processes of democratisation. Neo-classical economic theories are now being adapted to construct a 'new growth theory' which re-introduces a role for government policy in promoting the conditions necessary for long-term growth and development.[6] It is in this context that the World Bank could make the statement quoted at the opening of this chapter, with its neo-liberal emphasis on the individual being freed from the constraints of the state in order to take responsibility for meeting his or her own needs.

From the left of the political spectrum, theorising on development in the 1960s and 1970s proliferated. Approaches included the structuralism of the UN Economic Commission for Latin America, dependency theories, and world-systems theory. There was much emphasis on policy designed to encourage the development of industry and commerce within less developed countries through the replacement of imported goods with locally produced goods (import substitution), which was supposed to lead to industrialisation and locally generated economic growth. By the 1980s, however, these theories were generally discredited, particularly because of the rapid growth and industrialisation taking place in the so-called 'Newly Industrialising Countries' (NICs) such as South Korea, Taiwan, and Singapore, based on the export of mass-produced consumer goods. Many theorists of the left felt that an impasse had been reached.[7] The collapse of the Soviet Union and the ending of the Cold War presented a further challenge to left-wing thinking. Post-modernist theories have provided another challenge, with a new emphasis on diversity and the politics of difference.[8] Increasingly, the whole concept of development itself is being questioned: 'developmentalism' is seen as a Western imposition which forces non-Western countries into a particular set of economic priorities which may be inappropriate to their needs.[9] So in the 1980s and 1990s there has been a switch in emphasis towards empirical and local-level analysis, and a greater focus on practical issues. It is not surprising, therefore, to find a growing emphasis on the work of NGOs and grassroots organisations in the literature of the political left.

This new thinking on development has begun to be incorporated into theories and practical approaches to development on the part of NGOs and grassroots organisations. For example, in the area of credit provision to the poor, practical measures for targeting particular groups and managing funds, originating in India and Bangladesh, have been widely disseminated.[10] There is a growing interest in 'bottom-up' development, (as opposed to the dominant 'top-down' approach that was the legacy of modernisation theory and the now largely discredited but remarkably tenacious model which assumed that wealth generated by industrialists, large-scale entrepreneurs or state investments would somehow 'trickle-down' to the poorer sections of the population).[11] Terms such as 'participation', 'consultation', and 'partnership' began to enter the development vocabulary, reflecting the increased importance being given by many development organisations to an enabling approach which respects people's abilities to identify and express their own needs and priorities.[12] It also indicates a commitment to change practices based on neo-colonial attitudes that perpetuate relations of inequality. The term 'empowerment' has also arisen within this context.

Women and gender

In parallel to, and influencing, the debates on development theory has been the emergence of theories concerned with women and development and, later, gender and development.

Women in Development (WID)

Initiated by the ground-breaking work of Esther Boserup, the Women in Development (WID) school provided a powerful critique from a liberal feminist perspective of development theories which concentrated on men as producers and household heads, and completely ignored women except in their roles as housewives and mothers, seeing women as simply recipients of welfare.[13] WID units were established within agencies, seeking to bring women into development, mainly by including women's components in wider development projects and programmes. The assumption was that if women were 'made visible' and included in the development process, and there was a change of policy from welfare provision to equality, women would no longer be marginalised, and everyone would benefit. As neo-liberal approaches to economic development became popular, the integration of women into development was also seen as an 'efficient' approach that utilised women's productive potential.[14]

This approach did not question the existing social structures or the causes of women's subordination, focusing instead on women's role in production. It was (and continues to be) an approach which 'instrumentalises' women, using them as a resource for meeting other development goals such as population control, sustainable development, and so on.[15] Marxist feminist critics of WID argued that women have always been a part of development processes, but that they have been 'invisible' because of structural inequalities in society.[16]

Gender and Development (GAD)

In the late 1970s and 1980s a new analysis emerged which considered the interactions of women's various roles with those of men. Gender and Development (GAD), as it became known, is an approach concerned with the dynamics of gender relations. Women, for example, are housewives in a social context where men and other women expect them to be housewives. Gender relations are seen as central to social processes and social organisation (though not as their only important feature), and therefore to development, which is defined as 'a complex process involving the social, economic, political and cultural betterment of individuals and of society itself'.[17] GAD theorists have highlighted the value systems which lead to a sexual division of labour.

An analysisof the processes by which gender relations are negotiated and re-negotiated can assist in understanding the nature of households, of the constitution of the labour force, of the 'informal' economy, and other basic constructs of development analysis. Gender analysis which takes account of the diversity of people's circumstances, moves beyond the simple dichotomies of public/private, formal/informal, urban/rural, and production/reproduction to include women's physical situation, relationships within the household, health, sexuality, education, means of livelihood and so on, since gender inequalities touch all aspects of women's lives. In particular, a GAD approach illuminates the power relations between men and women, and the situation of subordination that most women face in most societies. Gender analysis also provides a critique of supposedly neutral institutions[18] and reveals the many manifestations of male bias[19] in the development process.

A difficulty in practice with the GAD approach, as with WID, is that gender can be used in an instrumentalist way to facilitate other objectives within the prevailing ideologies: 'gender' can become a proxy for 'women', who are then used as the vehicles through which some policy can be fulfilled. So, for example, a focus on women heads of household as beneficiaries might be put forward as a way to tackle the issue of women's non-involvement in a project. That may well increase women's participation in quantitative terms. It is very likely, however, that women's workload will have been increased; the onus is on women to make the changes in their activity patterns in order to become involved. But the gender issues of women's non-participation are complex, and targeting women in this way may mean that fundamental questions about gender relations in society are not asked. For example, why is the incidence of women as heads of household increasing? Why is the division of responsibility for domestic and reproductive activity apportioned in a way that makes women's burden so heavy? Why is work not being done with men towards changing the nature of men's participation so that women are more able to become involved? Tackling economic issues in this way also leaves untouched other, uncomfortable, pressures on women, such as domestic violence and abandonment, that affect not only their economic or project participation, but also their other activities and responsibilities and their general well-being. These gender issues affect women's lives at least as profoundly as their lack of access to credit or training opportunities. Superficial categorisation of women and women's needs also excludes the needs of women who are not household heads, who are rendered invisible within male-headed households.

Women and empowerment

The notion of the empowerment of women has increasingly become a part of the gender and development debate over the past ten years. Caroline Moser identified the 'empowerment approach' to gender planning.[20] Whereas the 'welfare', 'equity' 'efficiency' and 'anti-poverty' approaches might come out of a WID analysis, the 'empowerment approach' can arise from a GAD perspective, perhaps combined with bottom-up or 'actor-oriented' strategies. The focus on empowerment has been strengthened by the distinction, useful for analysis and planning, between women's practical and strategic gender interests.[21] Women's practical needs result from their position[22] in society; that position means that women also have strategic needs, that challenge the gender hierarchies and other mechanisms of subordination.[23] Although practical and strategic interests and needs may not be as clearly separable as most of the literature implies,[24] the distinction has made it possible to think about how to address gender and development issues in a pragmatic way without losing sight of the fundamental changes required to tackle gender inequalities.[25] Eliminating male bias and moving women out of the condition of near-universal subordination they still currently occupy will not be achieved by tinkering with conditions of employment or national accounting procedures; it will require cultural, economic and political changes. The power dynamics between men and women will have to be addressed.

The terminology of empowerment has arisen, however, not only from theoretical debate, but out of the practical experiences of women working at the grassroots level in many parts of the world. Significant contributions to the thinking behind the empowerment approach have come from Third World women.[26] Debates on the issue have been continuing in South Asia and the Philippines, among development practitioners and grassroots activists in their search for effective ways of supporting women and enabling them to make changes.[27]

Defining empowerment

In general, the meaning of the term 'empowerment', in either a development or a gender context, is not very precise. The word tends to be used in a way which presupposes that the reader or listener will know what is meant, and that the question of how empowerment comes about can either be assumed or ignored. The term may be used merely to communicate good intentions, and to imply some unspecified recognition of the need for changes in the distribution of power.

7

To take some random examples: Chambers talks about 'enabling and empowering poor clients'[28] and discusses the need for service organisations to 'see that clients know their rights and have power to demand them, enabling them to ensure quality of service and access'.[29] But how? Of what does the crucial process of getting to that point consist for those poor clients? Wasserstrom talks of the Inter-American Foundation's focus on the 'delicate and challenging task of *empowerment*, of helping poor people to create viable organisations of their own'.[30] Because no clear explanation of empowerment is given, it then becomes possible to sustain a notion of empowerment as something that can be done 'to' people, an issue we will return to later in the book.

Unless empowerment is given a more concrete meaning, it can be ignored, or used to obscure, confuse or divert debates.[31] The failure to define and explore the practical details of how empowerment can be achieved considerably weakens the value of the concept as a tool for analysis or as part of a strategy for change. In the next chapter I will therefore begin the process of defining and exploring the idea of empowerment more precisely.

2

Power and empowerment

How can it be that people and organisations as far apart politically as feminists, Western politicians, and the World Bank have all embraced the concept of empowerment with such enthusiasm? The profound — but often unrecognised — differences in the ways in which power is understood can help to explaining this anomaly. Views about the term can be polarised: in interviews with senior British NGO staff, Dolan found that 'Empowerment was a term avoided by some interviewees as being dangerously political, but embraced by others as the key to meaningful development'.[1]

The use of the term in some disciplines — adult education, community work, health and social work in particular — is relatively advanced, though here too there is a need for greater clarity about the concept and its application. 'Empowerment' is also used in a business management context, where it is becoming rather fashionable to talk of employee empowerment. On the whole, users of the term tend to assume an understanding of the appropriate meaning within a particular context.

To try to come closer to an understanding of empowerment, we need to look at actual examples of how the term, and its root-concept, power, have been used by writers and researchers, in a variety of contexts.

What is power?

Some of the confusion about empowerment arises because the root-concept — power — is itself disputed. Power has been the subject of much debate across the social sciences.[2] Some definitions focus, with varying degrees of subtlety, on the ability of one person or group to get another person or group to do something against their will. Such power could be described as 'zero-sum': the more power one person has, the less the other has. Thus, if person A and person B want things which are incompatible, and person A gets his or her way, then power has been exercised by A. This kind of power can be seen in operation at many levels, from the household to national or international policy making. It can be expressed in extreme form as violence or other kinds of force (or the threat of it), but it can be associated with other forms of interaction. For example, extra resources may be offered, or resources may be taken away (or the threat to do so made) in exchange for certain behaviour that would not otherwise be forthcoming.

Power and conflict

Conflict, however, is not always overt, and the reasons for decisions are not always easily visible. A powerful group might create a set of 'rules of the game' that effectively prevent a less powerful group from voicing its wishes. 'Non-decision making' — a decision not to do something, perhaps not to object — may also result from the exercise of power. Thus manipulation, misinformation, and other ways of exerting influence are examples of the exercise of power, since they suppress what would otherwise have been open conflict.

Steven Lukes argued that power is not only being exercised in the observable areas of conflict or suppressed conflict described above, but also in 'unobservable conflict'.[3] He argued that the supreme effect of power is to prevent people from even thinking of having the conflict:

the most effective and insidious use of power is to prevent ... conflict arising in the first place ... by shaping [people's] perceptions, cognitions and preferences in such a way that they accept their role in the existing order of things, either because they can see or imagine no alternative to it, or because they see it as natural and unchangeable or because they value it as divinely ordained and beneficial (p23-4).

Conflict can thus be prevented by making it impossible for people to imagine anything different from the status quo, or by perceiving it as natural or as divinely inspired. Such unobservable conflict is between A's interests and the interests B would have were B in a position to think clearly and articulate B's own 'real' interests. For Lukes, therefore, power is still concerned with decision making and conflict, but these can be invisible and latent.

A gender analysis of power

Most frameworks for understanding power are apparently neutral: they make no comment about how power is distributed within a society. There is no consideration of the power dynamics of gender, or of race, class, or any other force of oppression. This omission is redressed by a number of feminist theorists.[4]

People who are systematically denied power and influence in society internalise the messages they receive about what they are supposed to be like, and they may come to believe the messages to be true.[5] This 'internalised oppression' is an example of Lukes' 'unobservable conflict'. It may be adopted as a survival mechanism. Thus, for example, a woman who is subjected to violent abuse when she expresses her opinions may start to withhold them, and eventually come to believe that she has no opinions of her own. When control becomes internalised in this way, it is no longer necessary to assert power overtly.

If power is defined as 'power over', a gender analysis shows that power is wielded predominantly by men over other men, and by men over women. Extending this analysis to other forms of social differentiation, power is exercised by dominant social, political, economic, or cultural groups over those who are marginalised. Power, in this sense, is in finite supply; if some people have more, others have less.

This is a crucial issue. When power is defined as 'power over', then if women gain power it will be at men's expense. It is easy to see why the notion of women becoming empowered is seen as inherently threatening, the assumption being that there will be some kind of reversal of relationships, and men will not only lose power but also face the possibility of having power wielded over them by women. Men's fear of losing control is an obstacle to women's empowerment. But is it necessarily an outcome of women's empowerment that men should lose power; and, further, should a loss of power be something to fear?

Power within development discourse

A particular view of 'development-as-Westernisation' has come to dominate development discourse to such an extent that is has become virtually impossible to imagine any different form of development. Empowerment, in this context, is constructed on a 'power over' definition of power: women should somehow be empowered to participate within the economic and political structures of society. They should be given the chance to occupy positions of power, in terms of political and economic decision-making. This view of empowerment is consistent with the dictionary definition, which focuses on delegation: on power as something which can be bestowed by one person upon another. The difficulty with this interpretation is that if power can be bestowed, it can just as easily be withdrawn; empowerment as a gift does not involve a structural change in power relations.

Power as process

There are, however, other ways of understanding and conceptualising power, which focus on *processes*. When power is defined as 'power to', 'power with', and 'power from within', this entails very different meanings for empowerment. Nancy Hartsock (1985) contrasts the obedience definition of power with what she calls an 'energy' definition of power.[6] This is power which does not involve domination but is generative; for example, 'the power some people have of stimulating activity in others and raising their morale' (p.223).

One aspect of this 'power to' is the kind of leadership that comes from the wish to see a group achieve what it is capable of, where there is no conflict of interests, and the group is setting its own collective agenda. This model of power is not a zero-sum: an increase in one person's power does not necessarily diminish that of another. Liz Kelly (1992) observes: 'I suspect it is "power to" that the term "empowerment" refers to, and it is achieved by increasing one's ability to resist and challenge "power over".'[7]

Foucault's view of power

The French philosopher Foucault uses a different model of power. For him, power is not a finite entity that can be located, nor a substance of which people can possess more or less; power is relational and exists only in its exercise. It is constituted in a network of social relationships among subjects who are, to at least a minimal extent, free to act.[8] He sees power as a 'mode of action upon actions'. His is a notion of power as productive and intimately bound up with knowledge. Foucault's model includes an understanding of resistance as a form of power. His focus is mainly on micro-politics: the local exercise of power at particular points, and the resistance to it. Foucault does not allow for the internal processes which can interfere with the individual's agency and choice. He does not seem to conceive of any relationship where the individual is not 'acting on' another, and he therefore does not account for more than one individual joining together to act with each other:

Foucault's power analysis prevents us from seeing or conceptualising relationships in which the object is neither to act upon another in a power relation or to resist the attempts of governing conduct or a local manifestation of power; [Foucault's analysis] is a framework that seems inappropriate for describing co-operative efforts aimed both at political transformation and personal empowerment or consciousness-raising.[9]

A feminist model of power, then, would draw on the thinking of Foucault, but would incorporate a gender analysis of power relations that includes not only the more tangible expressions of power, but also an understanding of how internalised oppression creates barriers to women's exercise of power, thereby contributing to the maintenance of inequality between men and women;[10] and to the way in which male violence against women conditions women's experience.

Different forms of power

In order to understand the process of empowerment, we therefore need to be aware that power can take many different forms:

- **power over**: controlling power, which may be responded to with compliance, resistance (which weakens processes of victimisation)[11] or manipulation

- **power to**: generative or productive power (sometimes incorporating or manifesting as forms of resistance or manipulation) which creates new possibilities and actions without domination

- **power with**: 'a sense of the whole being greater than the sum of the individuals, especially when a group tackles problems together'[12]

- **power from within**: 'the spiritual strength and uniqueness that resides in each one of us and makes us truly human. Its basis is self-acceptance and self-respect which extend, in turn, to respect for and acceptance of others as equals.'[13]

What is empowerment?

Having considered some of the different manifestations of power, we can return to the question of what is meant by empowerment. Using the conventional definition, of 'power over', empowerment is bringing people who are outside the decision-making process into it. This puts a strong emphasis on participation in political structures and formal decision-making and, in the economic sphere, on the ability to obtain an income that enables participation in economic decision-making. Individuals are empowered when they are able to maximise the opportunities available to them without constraints.

Within the generative, 'power to' and 'power with', interpretation of power, empowerment is concerned with the processes by which people become aware of their own interests and how those relate to the interests of others, in order both to participate from a position of greater strength in decision-making and actually to influence such decisions.

Feminist interpretations of power lead to a still broader understanding of empowerment, since they go beyond formal and institutional definitions of power, and incorporate the idea of 'the personal as political'.[14] From a feminist perspective, interpreting 'power over' entails understanding the dynamics of oppression and internalised oppression. Empowerment is thus more than participation in decision-making; *it must also include the processes that lead people to perceive themselves as able and entitled to make decisions.* The feminist understanding of empowerment includes 'power to' and 'power from within'. It involves giving scope to the full range of human abilities and potential. As feminist and other social theorists have shown, societies ascribe a particular set of abilities to social categories of people. Empowerment must involve undoing negative social constructions, so that people come to see themselves as having the capacity and the right to act and influence decisions.

Figure 1 The three dimensions of empowerment

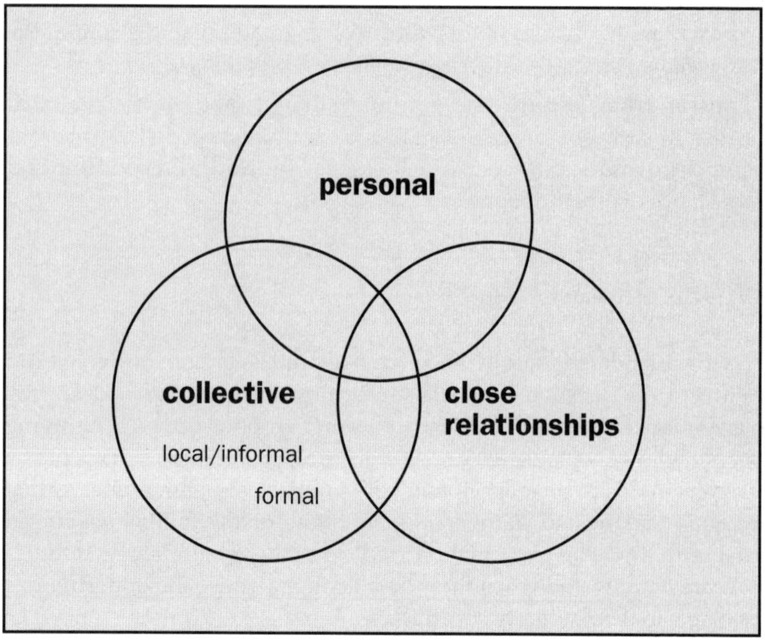

personal

collective

close relationships

local/informal

formal

The dimensions of empowerment

How is empowerment experienced and demonstrated? This wider picture shows empowerment to be operating within three dimensions:

- **personal**: developing a sense of self and individual confidence and capacity, and undoing the effects of internalised oppression

- **relational**: developing the ability to negotiate and influence the nature of a relationship and decisions made within it

- **collective**: where individuals work together to achieve a more extensive impact than each could have had alone. This includes involvement in political structures, but might also cover collective action based on co-operation rather than competition. Collective action may be locally focused — for example, groups acting at village or neighbourhood level — or be more institutionalised, such as the activities of national networks or the formal procedures of the United Nations.

I will now turn to the use of 'empowerment' within the fields of social work and education, where the term is in wide circulation; then consider its use by writers and researchers on development.

Empowerment in the context of social work and education

There is broad agreement within these disciplines that empowerment is a process; that it involves some degree of personal development, but that this is not sufficient; and that it involves moving from insight to action.

In a counselling context, McWhirter defines empowerment as:

*The **process** by which people, organisations or groups who are powerless (a) become aware of the power dynamics at work in their life context, (b) develop the skills and capacity for gaining some reasonable control over their lives, (c) exercise this control without infringing upon the rights of others and (d) support the empowerment of others in the community.* [15]

She distinguishes between 'the situation of empowerment', where all four of these conditions are met; and 'an empowering situation', where one or more of the conditions is in place or being developed, but where the full requirements are not present. Understanding your situation is important; if you do, you are more likely to act to change it. McWhirter's definition makes it clear that taking action is not about gaining the power to dominate others.

Writers on social group work also insist that empowerment must be used in the context of oppression, since empowerment is about working to remove the existence and effects of unjust inequalities.[16] Empowerment can take place on a small scale, linking people with others in similar situations through self-help, education, support, or social action groups and network building; or on a larger scale, through community organisation, campaigning, legislative lobbying, social planning, and policy development.[17]

The definitions of empowerment used in education, counselling, and social work, although developed through work in industrialised countries, are broadly similar to Freire's concept of *conscientisation*, which centres on individuals becoming 'subjects' in their own lives and developing a 'critical consciousness' — that is, an understanding of their circumstances and the social environment, that leads to action.

In practice, much empowerment work involves forms of group work. The role of the outside professional in this context becomes one of helper and facilitator; anything more directive is seen as interfering with the empowerment of the people concerned. The outside professional cannot expect to control the outcomes of authentic empowerment. Writing about education, Taliaferro (1991) points out that true power cannot be bestowed: it comes from within. Any notion of empowerment being 'given' by one group to another hides an attempt to keep control; and she describes the idea of gradual empowerment as 'especially dubious'. Real empowerment may take unanticipated directions. Outside professionals should therefore be clear that any 'power over' which they have in relation to the people they work with is likely to be challenged.

This raises an ethical and political issue: if one party has more power — as is the case with statutory authorities or financially powerful organisations, such as development agencies in respect of groups they support — it is misleading to deny that this is so. This point is relevant for development professionals and will be returned to in chapter 7.

Theories of empowerment in development literature

Empowerment is necessary for poor and marginalised people if they are to change their situation. Much of what has been written about empowerment originates from work in industrialised societies. Do poor or otherwise marginalised women and men experience similar problems in developing countries? In both cases, their lack of resources and formal power is significant; McWhirter's definition of empowerment seems equally relevant to either context. Any difference is more likely to show up in the particular activities that are called for. This is confirmed in one of the few definitions of empowerment which has a specific focus on development, in which it is described as:

*A process whereby women become able to organise themselves to increase
their own self-reliance, to assert their independent right to make choices and
to control resources which will assist in challenging and eliminating their
own subordination.*[18]

Here, control of resources is included as a goal, although that goal is
itself clearly part of a wider purpose.

Caroline Moser's definition of empowerment is similar, though
perhaps more focused on the individual. Control of resources is seen
more centrally as the means to an end. Empowerment is:

*the capacity of women to increase their own self-reliance and internal strength.
This is identified as the right to determine choices in life and to influence the
direction of change, through the ability to gain control over material and non-
material resources.*[19]

Janet Price argues that empowerment also 'moves beyond [personal
change and growth] to increasing participation in the broader field of
politics and needs-identification'.[20] This raises the question of the
relationship between an individual's internal sense of power and the
broader structures of society. The issue of who identifies women's needs
is also important, since in so many approaches to development, the
needs are identified by some outside body. In the case of SUTRA, an
Indian NGO, Price describes how women defining their own needs and
priorities was an essential part of the empowerment process.

Many usages of the terminology of empowerment within development literature are incidental and occur as part of accounts or debates on
other issues.[21] Some people, however, approach the subject more directly
and present more detail in their thinking. For example, Friedmann
explores further the meaning of empowerment in a development context
as a central part of his theory of 'alternative development'.[22] Basing his
analysis mainly on the household, he considers that households
potentially have three kinds of power: social power (in terms of information, knowledge, skills, financial resources and participation in social
organisations); political power (in terms of access to decisions affecting
their own future, whether through the vote, or through collective action);
and psychological power (in terms of the individual's sense of potency or
self-confidence). He sees the latter as coming out of the first two. The
alternative development he proposes 'seeks the empowerment of households and their individual members in all three senses'.[23]

Alan Thomas, in relation to the work of NGOs, is critical of attempts to
present empowerment as a model of development.[24] He identifies two
main empowerment approaches: that of 'tools for self-reliance',
associated with the ideas of E F Schumacher;[25] and that of participative
action research, associated in part with the ideas of Freire.[26] He portrays

both of these approaches as attempts to use the participation of local people as a route to the solution of local problems, seeing them as limited to particular situations and not easily replicable elsewhere. His portrayal of empowerment, whilst more detailed than most, does not enter into a discussion of what empowerment consists of, but focuses instead on the evident limitations of attempts at empowerment to date, including the structural limitations of NGOs and the reality that many local problems have causes well outside the immediate community.

Hazel Johnson, looking more specifically at women's empowerment in the context of the increase in women's organisations and collective activities in Latin America in recent years, writes that:

women's empowerment involves gaining a voice, having mobility and establishing a public presence. Although women can empower themselves by obtaining some control over different aspects of their daily lives, empowerment also suggests the need to gain some control over power structures, or to change them.[27]

She associates empowerment with the taking of some sort of *collective public action* beyond the individual on the basis of a collective class, gender or other identity, often based on the needs of family survival. For Johnson, empowerment is a process that may be very slow, involving self-discovery and the development of a collective identity. The public action that comes out of this process may challenge existing power structures, and may identify different development priorities.

The role of the 'professional' or the outsider in a development context is just as important as in the social work contexts referred to above. Price describes the crucial role played by local women staff of an Indian NGO, giving an example of how the account of a woman worker of her personal experiences of violence and mistreatment from her husband enabled women in the communities to overcome social taboos and speak of their own experiences. This is in stark contrast to the tendency in many development projects, as in Ngau's account of the Kenyan Harambee movement, for professional/client relationships to be fostered by para-professionals, fuelling resentment among local people.[28] This has implications for the way in which personnel in development programmes and projects — as well as in aid agencies — perform their work, which will be considered in detail in chapter 7.

Salil Shetty, in an exploration of the literature of the assessment of empowerment in development projects, concludes that 'no single definition of the term can do it justice.'[29] He proposes an analytical framework that includes the notion of empowerment as process: as a holistic approach that does not fit within a conventional project cycle, and is context-specific. He sees it as being chiefly related to 'strategic' aspects[30] with an emphasis on democratisation and sustainability. He highlights the psychological element of empowerment.

Shetty makes a distinction between empowerment at the 'group level', where he distinguishes between internal and external empowerment, and the 'individual/household level'. His account leaves the question of power untouched. He proposes the use of participatory methods in the assessment of empowerment, but although he is critical of the 'instrumentalist' approach of many projects, he fails to tackle the power relationships inherent in the project-oriented development.

Perhaps the most commonly cited work that relates to empowerment, and specifically to women's empowerment, is that of the DAWN network of Third World women theorists and activists.[31] They highlight the empowerment of women as of central importance in the slow process of social, political and economic change that is needed to turn the 'alternative visions' they present into reality. They emphasise the various ways in which organisations, through internal democratic and participatory processes, can contribute to women's empowerment.

I will now look in more detail at the way empowerment is dealt with by five writers, whose work is of particular relvance to my own research.

The 'Caribbean Women's Empowerment Wheel'

Jennifer Harold[32] developed her 'Caribbean Women's Empowerment Wheel' ('CariWheel') through a series of workshops with four organisations, where the object was for the participants to construct their own understanding of empowerment and then apply that to an analysis of the achievements and nature of their own organisations, identifying strengths and weaknesses (see Figure 2).

The CariWheel puts analysis of personal and group change into a social and political context. The wheels that make up her model represent action for change, vision for change, context, personal, and group change. The components of the 'personal' and 'group change' wheel include understanding of self and others, travel, support from others, friendship, making decisions, identifying needs, development of skills, and self-confidence. The 'action for change' wheel describes the immediate actions coming out of the inner wheel. The 'vision for social change' wheel represents the women's sense of what they are trying to achieve. Finally, the 'context' wheel represents some of the specific social conditions within which women in the Caribbean live, which 'join together to discourage the operation of empowerment'. Spirituality and sexuality are placed together at the centre of the 'CariWheel' as the base on which the wheels rest.

What is not clear from Harold's work is whether spirituality and sexuality are themselves necessary components of empowerment processes, or whether they provide a framework upon which some of the

Figure 2 Caribbean women's empowerment wheel

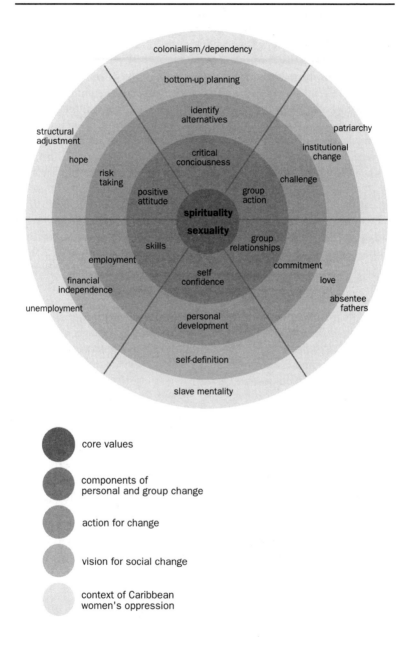

Adapted from Harold (1991)

component aspects can be developed — such as a sense of self-worth, or a sense of purpose. This is a debatable area which would need further research to establish, but which is receiving more serious attention of late.[33]

Harold's CariWheel is helpful in considering where a group perceives itself to be in relation to its own processes of empowerment; the methodology appears to have great potential for use with a wide variety of groups. As described in the evaluative comments of women who worked with it, the CariWheel is successful as an aid to systematisation and analysis. By avoiding a linear portrayal, and using the idea of wheels which can rotate to show relationships between many combinations of elements, Harold's model depicts movement and dynamism. However, it falls short of pinpointing the *processes* of empowerment, focusing instead on perceptions of degrees of empowerment and visions of what might be possible. In focusing predominantly on the collective dimension, the CariWheel does not make a connection between personal and collective empowerment. The model is therefore somewhat vulnerable to generalisation in areas where, to provide an effective analytical or planning tool, specifics are needed.

Harold's model enables a detailed discussion of the possible ingredients of empowerment but not of why empowerment occurs, nor how it could be achieved. This may not be such a serious problem for a group using the CariWheel to assist its own internal processes, since these will be in the context of the group's other activities and planning processes. As a framework for assisting the design of supportive interventions by an outside body, however, it is of more limited use.

Building on 'power within': the work of Naila Kabeer

Another dynamic account of empowerment has recently been provided by Naila Kabeer[34] in a book which examines critically many aspects of development in relation to gender. Kabeer regards empowerment as a concept with theoretical and practical potential that merits being more than an empty slogan. She found it necessary to deconstruct the notion of power in order to consider empowerment. She reasons that:

The multidimensional nature of power suggests that empowerment strategies for women must build on 'the power within' as a necessary adjunct to improving their ability to control resources, to determine agendas and make decisions. (p.229)

Power from within needs 'experiential recognition and analysis' of issues to do with women's own subordination and how it is maintained. 'Such power cannot be given; it has to be self-generated'.(p.229)

Kabeer does not attempt to develop a specific framework, but uses examples of NGOs and grassroots organisations in South Asia to explore attempts to promote empowerment. In relation to the Grameen Bank in Bangladesh, and SEWA and SUTRA in India, she discusses the importance of providing an opportunity for women's views to be heard, emphasising participatory processes of needs-identification. She highlights the

interdependency between different categories of needs, particularly in the lives of women. ... (W)hat occurs in any one arena will have implications for all other arenas, sometimes to the extent of negating the intended effects of an intervention. (p.234)

She suggests that the 'bottom-up' identification of needs conveys a positioning of women as 'competent, but socially constrained actors who are capable of making choices, articulating priorities and taking responsibility' (p.235). Innovative NGOs have sought to work with women 'as agents and participants in the development effort rather than as clients and recipients. This has entailed an emphasis on building a sense of ownership and responsibility among poor women in relation to the organisation's activities'.

She also identifies the expansion of women's mobility as a significant feature: 'such travel plays an important role in breaking down the sense of isolation and powerlessness that women are often trapped in.'(p.251)

Naila Kabeer's work emphasises the importance of such elements as self-respect, and the sense of agency, in empowerment processes, and also the building of organisational capacity through conscious processes, support for leadership development, and the strengthening of networks. There is a strong focus on the collective dimension as an adjunct to personal empowerment:

From a state of powerlessness that manifests itself in a feeling of 'I cannot', empowerment contains an element of collective self-confidence that results in a feeling of 'we can'.[35]

She sees analysis and reflection as crucial:

New forms of consciousness arise out of women's newly acquired access to the intangible resources of analytical skills, social networks, organisational strength, solidarity and sense of not being alone. (p.245-6)

Kabeer stresses the need to move beyond project participation into the realm of policy making. The state, civil society, and economic structures all shape and constrain women's lives; and any changes that are achieved are made in the context of those powerful forces. She concludes that:

the longer-term sustainability of empowerment strategies will depend on the extent to which they envision women struggling within a given set of policy priorities and the extent to which they empower them to challenge and reverse these priorities. It is only when the participation of poorer women goes beyond participation at the project level to intervening in the broader policy making agenda that their strategic interests can become an enduring influence on the course of development. (p.262)

Kabeer confines her analysis predominantly to grassroots NGOs, and does not enter into the micro-level analysis of empowerment for the individual woman; her account therefore misses the intricate interactions between personal, collective, and relational dimensions of empowerment.

Empowerment, economics, and development: the work of Srilatha Batliwala

Srilatha Batliwala[36] has made a detailed analysis of women's empowerment programmes in South Asia, looking at integrated rural development (IRD: economic interventions, awareness-building, and organising of women) and at research, training, and resource support.

She notes that in some (especially IRD) programmes, the terms *empowerment* and *development* are used synonymously. It is often assumed that power comes automatically through economic strength. It may do, but often it does not, depending on specific relations determined by gender, culture, class, or caste. Economic activities do not always improve women's economic situation, and often add extra burdens. Often, development work is still done 'for' women, and an exclusive focus on economic activities does not encourage women to look at their gender roles, or other aspects of their lives. Batliwala takes empowerment to mean, in part, the 'exercise of *informed choice* within an expanding framework of information, knowledge and analysis'(p.7); 'a process which must enable women to discover new possibilities, new options.....a growing repertoire of choices'(p.11).

Batliwala distinguishes between personal and collective empowerment; she describes the process of empowerment as a spiral rather than a cycle, which affects all the people involved in that change, including any change agent: 'Empowerment is thus not merely a change of mind-set, but a visible demonstration of ... change which the world around is forced to acknowledge, respond to, and accommodate as best it may.'(p.10) She points out that empowerment is a process that involves a redistribution of power, particularly within the household. She highlights 'the widespread fear that women's empowerment is against men', and argues that

women's empowerment, if it is a real success, does mean the loss of men's traditional power and control over the women in their households: control of her body and her physical mobility; the right to abdicate from all responsibility for housework and the care of children; the right to physically abuse or violate her; the right to spend family income on personal pleasures (and vices); the right to abandon her or take other wives; the right to take unilateral decisions which affect the whole family; and the countless other ways in which poor men — and indeed men of every class — have unjustly confined women. (p.9)

She goes on to say, 'the point that is often missed, however, is that *the process of women's empowerment will also liberate men* ... They will be relieved of gender stereotyping, just like women'.

Batliwala draws on the wealth of experience of the various organisations involved in the workshop on which her work is based, to analyse three broad approaches to women's empowerment, outlining the strategies involved and the possible indicators of empowerment, and discussing the dilemmas and limitations of each approach. 'Empowerment through integrated rural development (IRD)' is seen as a functional approach, not differing much except in terminology from conventional IRD approaches. 'Empowerment through economic interventions' isseen to assume that women's powerlessness arises from their weak position economically, and that that is the only factor; solutions using this approach often merely add to women's work burdens. 'Empowerment through awareness-building and organising women' is the approach that most directly equates with the model of empowerment which I developed from my research in Honduras. The strategies identified for this approach revolve around the training of change agents (from within or outside the community); building women's groups; developing critical consciousness through dialogues, discussion and analysis, about structures of inequality and other problems raised by women; and enabling women to acquire new information and skills.

She believes it is important to begin with 'the women's own experiences and realities [to] promote self-recognition and positive self-image, stimulate critical thinking and deepen understanding of the structures of power, including gender' and to enable women 'to identify and prioritise issues for action, based on expanding awareness (including new information, knowledge) critical analysis and informed decision making', and then to encourage women 'to *independently* struggle for changes in their material conditions of existence, their personal lives and their treatment in the "public" sphere'.(p.13) Support for women acting to meet their own needs, through schemes to generate income or provide credit, and the creation of women's organisations and networks are other important strategies. Batliwala is clear that empowerment has to include the action element as well as the changes in awareness and self-image.

In assessing this approach to empowerment, Batliwala indicates a factor that makes it less attractive to agencies working with women: it can be slow, taking longer than other approaches to have visible results. Changes in women's economic position or health status may take some time to happen, and participants become discouraged. Batliwala points out that, to tackle these difficulties, women 'feel that some judicious mix of both the "concrete" and "abstract" elements of empowerment is necessary to make a broader impact on poor women's life situation' and that:

the design of these interventions has to be very different from that used in the developmental approach: i.e. be it an income generation program, alternate health service, or functional literacy class, it must be conceived, planned and operationalised under women's — not NGO — control. For genuine empowerment to occur, women should not become passive recipients or beneficiaries, but, over time, the 'owners' of the program, so that they can eventually run it without the support of any outside agency. (p.36)

Batliwala is critical of non-directive, open-ended approaches, such as 'empowerment through awareness building and organising women', because they are strong on soft issues and weak on hard issues. But this criticism itself reveals an unwillingness to trust that women, through processes of empowerment, become able to set their own priorities which, may or may not be the priorities that others would want or expect them to have.

Empowerment and conflict: Nira Yuval-Davis's critique

Nira Yuval-Davis takes a more openly critical stance of notions of empowerment than other writers.[37] She points out that empowerment for one group of people might easily represent another group's disempowerment, particularly if categories such as 'community' or 'women' are used in a way that does not allow for the existence of power relationships within such categories as well as between them and other categories. There may be serious conflicts of interest to be overcome. Empowerment cannot, therefore, be assumed to be non-problematic.

She also argues that 'empowerment of the oppressed, whether one fights for one's own — individual or group — sake, or that of others, cannot by itself be the goal for feminist and other anti-oppression politics', giving the example of the brutality and violence that was so common within the US Black Panther movement. She is cautious of constructions which 'assume a specific "identity politics" which homogenizes and naturalizes social categories and groupings, denying shifting boundaries and internal power differences and conflicts of interest'. Any notion of 'the empowerment of women' should therefore be approached critically.

Yuval-Davis cautions against allowing subjective feelings of empowerment to become the full criterion for evaluating a particular situation, citing the example of women who become involved in fundamentalist movements and gain a sense of empowerment from them, despite the way in which fundamentalist politics have made women their primary victims. These arguments are particularly relevant in considering how an analysis of empowerment may be used. It could be a tool for opening up discussions of similarity and difference and for negotiation, or it could be used to obscure areas of difference. It is important to remember that the process of analysis itself is not neutral.

Individual change and collective action: the work of Kate Young

Kate Young is another author who has recently written on empowerment.[38] She puts particular emphasis on the importance of seeing empowerment as a collective undertaking, involving 'both individual change and collective action'. She observes that the use of the term in mainstream development refers to 'entrepreneurial self-reliance' in a very individualistic sense; whereas the approach of collective empowerment based on co-operation will require changes in the power dynamics between men and women:

Just as women must organise together to gain the sense of self-worth and understanding of the wider context of their lives that empower and make long-term co-operation possible, so must men undergo a process of reflection and transformation which makes it possible for them to recognise the ways in which power is a double-edged sword. It structures their relations with other men in competition and conflict, and makes co-operation and building on advances highly problematic.

She concludes that 'both women and men need to change if future society is to be more harmonious than in the past.' Young's account does not identify the nature of power involved in the various approaches to empowerment, but she is clear that a sole focus on individual empowerment cannot effect significant changes in women's power within society. While personal empowerment is one ingredient in achieving empowerment in the collective dimension, whether informally or formally, concentration on the personal dimension alone is not sufficient; neither does personal empowerment automatically lead to empowerment within relationships.

For an empowerment approach to development to be successfully implemented, changes are needed in the abilities of individuals and groups to identify and meet their own needs, as households, communities, organisations, institutions, and societies. For women's empowerment, this means:

to take control of their own lives to set their own agendas, to organise to help each other and make demands on the state for support and on society itself for change. With the collective empowerment of women the direction and processes of development would also be shifted to respond to women's needs and their vision. The collective empowerment of women of course, would bring with it the individual empowerment of women, but not only for individual advancement. (p.159)

Conclusion

This review of empowerment shows that the concept can be of value in terms of organising and planning development interventions in a way that ensures that the needs of women are met;[39] but that its current usage reveals a range of definitions.

The case studies presented in chapters 4 and 5 were undertaken to support the development of a clearer definition (or clearer definitions) of empowerment by looking at work which is actually being done with women and its results, as well as to provide examples of the practice of empowerment and its effects on women's lives. I wanted to find out how the rhetoric of development translated into reality; to find out how empowerment happened, and why: what were the factors which actively encouraged it, and what influences had the effect of inhibiting its development.

Figure 3 A map of Honduras, showing places mentioned in this book

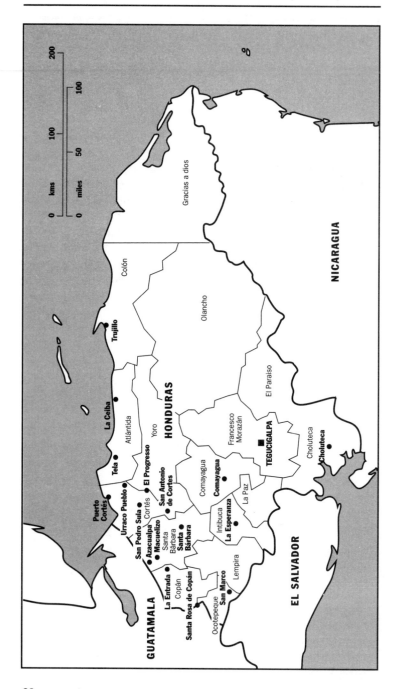

3

Background information on Honduras

The two case studies used in chapters 4 and 5 to explore empowerment are from Honduras. This chapter gives a brief overview of the historical, political, social, and economic circumstances of Honduras, and then looks in more detail at the situation of Honduran women. Honduras has much in common with its Central American neighbours, sharing a history of colonialism and neo-colonialism, and an economy dominated by plantation agriculture for the United States market. But Honduras is also very different from its neighbours in a number of significant ways, including the composition of its oligarchy, the nature of its trade-union movement, the absence of a significant guerrilla movement, and its strategic significance in terms of US foreign policy.

A history of domination

Although Honduras has a small population for the size of the country (5.4 million people in 1992[1] in an area of 112,492 square kilometres), the cultivable land is under great pressure, because much of the country is mountainous, and Honduras lacks the volcanic soils that make other Central American countries so fertile. The Honduran economy is nonetheless dominated by agriculture, and although there has been a steady rural–urban migration in the past two decades, about 60 per cent of the population lives in rural areas. The most fertile agricultural land is in the northern coastal area, and is given over to plantation agriculture dominated by the two big US fruit companies, United Brands (Chiquita) and Castle and Cooke (Standard Fruit/Dole), producing bananas and African palm.

Coffee has been grown since the 1940s, but Honduras previously lacked the infrastructure to gain access to world markets, and the stable rural population did not provide the flexible labour force required for large-scale coffee production. Honduras therefore was unable to benefit from the 'coffee boom' of the late nineteenth and early twentieth centuries enjoyed by other Central American countries.[2]

Export agriculture did not develop until the 1950s, when large landowners began to grow cotton and sugar, and some non-traditional crops such as pineapple and melon, and to expand beef production.[3] Seafood is an expanding new area of agro-exporting. However, the economy is still dependent on bananas for over a third of its export earnings. The majority of the rural population is reliant on self-provisioning agriculture, though the expansion of export agriculture is pushing peasant farmers on to more marginal land.

Industry, including manufacturing, does not play a very significant role in the Honduran economy, although its share of the Gross Domestic Product (GDP) is growing. Manufactured goods contribute about 20 per cent of export earnings. Forty per cent of Honduran manufacturing is artesanal in nature; the two big banana companies operate much of the factory-based manufacturing, producing plastics, cans, soap, cement, boxes, rubber, margarine, and vegetable oil. Export manufacturing grew during the 1970s and 1980s, aided by the Central American Common Market and the development of the Puerto Cortez Free Zone. By 1994, 45,000 people worked in the export processing sector; 20,000 jobs were created between 1990 and 1992, mostly in clothing assembly for duty-free re-import to the USA.[4]

Although Honduras has been influenced by the USA since the first involvement of the US fruit companies, it was with the overthrow of the Somoza regime in neighbouring Nicaragua in 1979 that Honduras took on a more central role in US foreign policy.[5] Under US pressure, Honduras ostensibly returned to civilian rule, giving the US a supposedly legitimate basis for providing significant military aid to a 'democracy' surrounded by countries in the throes of civil war (Guatemala and El Salvador) or under revolutionary government (Nicaragua). The US supported the Honduras-based Contra, the opposition to the Nicaraguan Sandinista regime. Direct military aid to Honduras between 1980 and 1989 was in the region of $442 million.[6] The US built a number of military bases in Honduras, as well as a large training facility, mainly used for training Salvadorean troops until it closed in 1985, and there have been many US/Honduran joint training exercises.

US influence on Honduras was not limited to military support. Economic aid between 1980 and 1989 was worth $1,143.4 million, and the

USA provides over 50 per cent of Honduran aid. US influence was also strong on the development of the trade union movement from the 1950s. Honduras was of prime strategic importance for US foreign policy throughout the Central American region.

Social structure and the position of the military

The population of Honduras is 90 per cent *mestizo* (mixed race), reflecting the history of domination. The remaining 10 per cent is made up of a number of indigenous groups, the largest being the Lenca, and the Garífuna, who have African/Caribbean origins. The population is also predominantly Catholic, although there is a growing membership of various Protestant churches.

It is very significant that in Honduras a strong local agrarian capitalist class failed to emerge and a middle class did not begin to develop until the 1950s. In other parts of Central America the introduction of export crops, and in particular coffee, in the second half of the nineteenth century, which linked economies to the world market, created powerful local elites. In Honduras, the major investors in export agriculture were foreign companies. Coffee is controlled by Hondurans, but is grown by between 30,000 and 40,000 small-scale independent producers.[7] In the absence of a ruling elite, Honduran society was controlled by local powerful individuals — *caudillos* — and by foreign capital.

The economic strength of the fruit companies, combined with the patronage system of *caudillismo*, have led to a poorly developed state structure, with the military as the only national institution of major significance. This has been reflected in the frequent changes in regime over the past century, with moves from civilian to military rule and back again, coups and counter-coups. Even the much vaunted 'return to democracy' of 1981 hid a continuing domination by the military. Massive US military aid enabled the military not only to develop the most powerful air force in the region but also to move into control of some key areas of the economy, including telecommunications, the cement industry, insurance, and banking.[8]

Military rule in Honduras did not take on the repressive characteristics of military rule elsewhere in the region. The Honduran military lacked its own strong organisational structures and relied heavily on a logistical alliance with the Nationalist Party.[9] Military rule was achieved mainly through negotiation and co-optation, with repression as a last resort. Law enforcement has been very unreliable; people without money have found it very difficult to pursue justice.

Politics and popular movements

Although ostensibly a multi-party democracy, Honduran politics have been dominated by two main parties since the 1890s. Both are right of centre, but the National Party (PN) is further to the political right than the Liberal Party (PL). The other two parties with legal status, the Christian Democratic Party (PDCH) and the Innovation and Unity Party (PINU), hold a handful of seats in Congress. The Honduran Communist Party (PCH) has never had legal status, and nor have its off-shoots. When elections are held, voting is largely still determined by *caudillismo*,[10] and the incoming party re-distributes government jobs among its own supporters, civilian or military. Political corruption is endemic.

Popular organisations and the trade union movement are well-established and influential. Plantation workers organised themselves at an early stage, and a strike in the plantations in 1954 spread to other parts of the country, closing down 60 per cent of the economy. A settlement was reached granting recognition to the more moderate unions, and this made it possible to organise workers throughout the country and sectors of the economy. The unions and the popular movements became a force to be reckoned with. This important development proved an opportunity for further US influence: Honduran unions received significant backing from the right-wing American Federation of Labor (AFL) and the associated Interamerican Regional Organisation of Labour (ORIT).[11] This support has ensured that the majority of trade union organisations in Honduras are moderate or right-wing, and popular organisations have become closely allied with some of the military governments.[12] The *campesino* (peasant) movement also developed during the 1950s, when many ex-plantation workers, who had been leased land or occupied it illegally when they lost their jobs, were being pushed off their land to make way for an expansion in cattle production.

A polarised economy

The Honduran economy is dominated by two extremes: peasant self-provisioning agriculture and multinational fruit companies. This is reflected in the distribution of wealth. In 1992 Honduras had a *per capita* GNP of US$580.[13] Of the population as a whole, the poorest 20 per cent have 5.5 per cent of the income, where the richest 20 per cent have 54.2 per cent.[14] Land ownership is very unequal, with 20 per cent of the productive land owned by a mere 279 landowners. In rural areas, 61 per cent of households lack piped water and 62 per cent lack sanitation; the infant mortality rate was 65 per thousand in 1985 (compared to an urban rate of 45 per thousand).[15] Research in 1987 revealed that approximately 50 per cent of households had inadequate intake of calories[16] and in 1993 some 20 per cent of children under five were found to be moderately or severely malnourished.[17]

External debt is a significant burden on the Honduran economy. The 1992 debt of US$3,573 million represented 92 per cent of GNP and 258.9 per cent of exports.[18] In 1990 the government introduced structural adjustment policies which succeeded in curbing inflation, but had a negative effect on the poorest because of the removal of subsidies on basic items.

The first Agrarian Reform legislation was introduced in 1962, but the land-owning *caudillos* and the fruit companies ensured that only public land could be redistributed. Further land reform legislation was enacted in 1972 by the liberal military regime of Colonel Lopez. This allowed 'unproductive' land to be expropriated from private as well as public ownership. However, even in the most active period of land transfer, government targets were not achieved, and much of the transfer that took place was in response to land invasions.[19] Land rights continue to be a significant issue for *campesino* organisations.

Addressing poverty and inequality in Honduras has become a major activity for a thriving array of Non-Government Development Organisations (NGDOs). In addition to official agencies such as the UNDP and UNICEF, there were an estimated 200 development organisations in 1988.[20] These vary widely, from church-run organisations to consultancies, from organisations running small-scale, 'shoestring' projects to ambitious Integrated Rural Development programmes. Large amounts of foreign aid are channelled through these organisations, and they provide a significant source of employment for the educated middle class, whose other main employment field, outside commerce and manufacturing, is the unreliable, politically-appointed government sector. There is much cynicism about NGDOs, which are often seen as providing 'jobs for the boys', and as being concerned with maximising job security and income for staff rather than meeting the needs of beneficiaries. Nonetheless, many organisations do excellent work, on their own or alongside government, and levels of infant mortality reduced and life-expectancy increased between 1985 and 1992.[21]

Women in Honduras

The situation of women in Honduras, and their position *vis-à-vis* men, is dominated by the location of Honduras within the global market economy and the patriarchal nature of Latin American society.[22] Honduran women contend with inequalities on many fronts.[23] The sexual division of labour leaves women carrying the burden of domestic and repro-ductive labour. Little paid work is available for women, and what there is is largely restricted to service industries and *maquila* (assembly plant) work. In urban areas there are more options for making a living, and far more women are economically active.

Honduran women are expected to fit into the gender role, common throughout Latin America, of wife-mother-maintainer of the home. To be a woman is to be long-suffering and resourceful; to carry the respons-ibility for the welfare of your children and often your partner. If women have ambitions these are generally expressed through hopes for their children and what the latter might achieve if they can attend school. Women endure with fatalism *machismo* and violence in various forms.

On paper, women have a strong position in Honduras. The govern-ment accepted the UN Charter abolishing all forms of discrimination against women that was a product of the International Decade for Women (1975-85) (although Honduran women were the last in Latin America to get the vote).[24] They have significant protection under the Family Code and the Labour Code, and in 1993 the Agricultural Modern-isation Law removed the blatant discrimination against women that had existed under the old Agrarian Reform Law. In 1989 a National Policy for Women was agreed. However, there is a large discrepancy between the theoretical rights women have and their actual situation in practice. The legal system and law enforcement are weak; and regulations and procedures to make the law operational are often missing. The social and cultural ethos of Honduras, heavily dominated by *machismo*, reinforces the subordinate position of women, and there is widespread ignorance among women of their legal rights.

An individual woman's situation is influenced by her socio-economic position, her stage in the life-cycle, and her relationship to the labour market. Whether she lives in a rural or urban area also makes a significant difference. The lives of most Honduran women are dominated by childbearing. Formal marriage is not necessary. Women are considered married to the first man with whom they have a sexual relationship. Many women have their first child at 15 or 16, and families with more than eight children are not unusual. The national average fertility rate is 5.98 children (6.72 for rural women and 5 for urban women). The fertility rate has declined from 7.2 in 1970 to 4.9 in 1992, according to a World Bank survey (World Bank, 1994). Maternal mortality is the principal cause of death among women between 15 and 40 years of age, at 2.2 deaths per thousand live births. The World Bank suggests that between 1988 and 1993, 47 per cent of married women (or their husbands) used contraception. (This is a misleading figure, given the high prevalence of *unión libre* (common-law) relationships in Honduras.[25] The Centre for Women's Studies (CEM) suggests that only 17.7 per cent of women of reproductive age use contraception.)[26] Health is a major issue for women. If a family member is ill it is up to the woman to care for them, and to try to get medical treatment if necessary. Caring for sick children is the most common reason for women to miss classes and meetings. The nutritional status both of the children and the parents is generally so poor that illness is common, and it lays a heavy burden on women. A large number of women are undernourished, a condition exacerbated by childbearing; data from the Secretariat of Public Health show that 42 per cent of women attending health centres suffer from anaemia,[27] and of lactating mothers 70 per cent have deficiencies in vitamin A and 15 per cent lack iodine.

Although there has been a 32 per cent drop in levels of women's illiteracy between 1974 and 1988,[28] over half of all women and more than two-thirds of rural women had received three years or fewer of formal education. Not surprisingly, there continue to be high levels of illiteracy among women, especially in the rural areas. More women now continue into secondary education, although mainly studying subjects that reflect women's traditional roles, such as secretarial studies, nursing, tailoring, and primary teaching.

Women comprise over a fifth of the recorded economically active population,[29] a significant increase over previous years (in 1974 the equivalent figure was 15.7 per cent). Some of the increase reflects better recording, but it is also likely to be a consequence of the need to maximise family income during a period of economic crisis. The majority of economically active women live in urban areas, and a large proportion are active in the informal sector.

Rural women have a low level of recorded participation in the agricultural labour force, although the production of basic grains absorbs nearly half of the rural workforce.[30] Under the Agrarian Reform law of 1974 women were not permitted to own land, except as widows with no sons; and, although the agricultural modernisation law of 1992 has altered that, it is unlikely that patterns of land ownership will change. Some women do succeed in getting access to land — perhaps lent by a co-operative or relative — but there are many stories of it being the least fertile land, or of land being taken back again as soon as women have made it productive. Some women help their husbands from time to time with work on the *milpa*, the family maize field, mostly at sowing and harvest time, but the dominant pattern is for women not to be involved in agriculture at all. Paid employment in agriculture for women is not widely available, with coffee harvesting (women are 12 per cent of the labour force in the main harvesting period) and banana packing (almost all the labour force is female) being the main sources. Women raise small animals, and grow vegetables and process agricultural products, for consumption or sale.[31] Until the Agricultural Modernisation law came into force in 1993, only 2 per cent of the members of agricultural co-operatives were female.[32] Because of the lack of opportunities for paid work in the rural areas, women are migrating to the cities at a faster rate than men; the majority of female migrants from the rural areas are single mothers and young women, hoping to find jobs in industry or as domestic servants.[33]

It has been estimated that, on average, rural women work 100 hours per week, including paid and unpaid work.[34] Their long day of activity is dominated by the requirements of child care and housework. The advent of mills for grinding maize for the staple *tortillas* have lightened the load for many women, though some women do not have access to one and others have to go quite a distance (one woman told me it took her half an hour by bicycle to get to the mill). The making of *tortillas* is still a very time-consuming activity that must be done at least once a day. In many villages women have to carry water from the well or river, and go to the river to do the washing. Hauling firewood for cooking is traditionally a man's job in Honduras; but for single women or their children, unless they can afford to buy firewood, this task also falls to them. Cooking is done on the traditional wood-burning stove used throughout Honduras: a raised platform made of mud, clay or occasionally, concrete, with a hole for the fire and a flat metal plate over it which provides the cooking surface. Improved fuel-efficient stoves are rarely used. Women are therefore exposed to wood smoke for long periods, and few of the houses have any chimney.

The adoption of structural adjustment policies in 1990 by the Callejas government brought a rise in prices, especially for basic foodstuffs. The policies have led to job losses and have adversely affected informal-sector sales. There have also been tax increases, and a rise in the costs of public services, as well as actual cuts to services. The impact on women, as primary carers for their families, has been severe, and they have adopted a wide range of strategies to cope with these problems. The government recognised the difficulties faced by women, particularly single parents, by setting up the Honduran Social Investment Fund (FHIS) to provide a package of investment in employment projects and other benefits, including a monthly payment of 20 Lempiras for single mothers with children of school age. Nearly one in four heads of households[35] are women, a significant increase on the one-fifth reported in the 1988 census.

Although there are no official figures on levels of violence, domestic or otherwise, against women in Honduras, there is no doubt that violence is a common feature of many women's lives. It is seen as a problem which is increasing, and the press often carry stories about it. The issue is recognised in the national policy for women.[36]

Women's organisations in Honduras.

The first women's organisation was the Sociedad de Cultura Feminina, Society of Feminine Culture, set up by Visitación Padilla in 1923.[37] In the late 1940s women's groups were formed to demand freedom for political prisoners. Women were actively involved in the 1954 strike, which was successful largely as a result of their efforts. Women organised communal kitchens which made it possible for the strikers to survive the 69-day ordeal. Their tactics also included closing bars and brothels to prevent men from spending money.[38] The second campaign during the 1950s was for women's enfranchisement. Some women who were related to men in positions of power were involved in this campaign, and this made possible the use of tactics such as public demonstrations that might otherwise have been repressed.

In the late 1960s, a network of 'housewives' clubs' (*clubes de amas de casa*) was set up in rural and urban areas. This was initially instigated by a private organisation with links with the Catholic church, but was soon taken over by CARITAS, the Catholic church's organisation concerned with social affairs.[39] The clubs were used for the distribution of donated food, partly through a 'food for work' programme. By 1974 there were about a thousand clubs throughout Honduras. The CARITAS programme was intended to help women to fulfil their traditional role, and was focused on health, nutrition, needlework, housing, and small productive projects. Women were given training and support through a network of promoters, who were local *campesina* women paid small daily allowances for their work.

In 1975 CARITAS stopped working with the housewives' clubs after the massacre in Los Horcones where priests, *campesinos*, and students were killed. This was part of a general withdrawal from activities considered too political. There were also differences of opinion within CARITAS. Some of the promoters decided to continue on a voluntary basis, with support from the National Campesino Union (UNC), and set up the Honduran Federation of Campesina Women (FEHMUC).

FEHMUC has concentrated on providing finance for women, in an attempt to incorporate women into the development process through economically productive projects. They have also provided training on health issues. They retained the organisational structure of base groups and promoters developed in the housewives' clubs, but now those women themselves were running the organisation. There were problems, however, with failed projects. FEHMUC's close relationship with UNC came under pressure because the UNC decided to establish their own programme with women and a women's affairs section, which each *campesino* organisation is required to have by law. Eventually the various internal conflicts became disruptive and in 1985 some leaders of FEHMUC most critical of the organisation, from the north and west of the country, were expelled. Another internal conflict led to a further division in 1989; this fluidity of organisational composition is not unusual among popular organisations and NGOs.

Some of the FEHMUC leaders expelled in 1985, having brought 'their' base groups with them, set up another organisation, CODIMCA (Council for the Integral Development of the Campesina Woman). CODIMCA works with women on organisation and training, with a particular focus on natural medicines. It has a similar organisational structure to FEHMUC, with national, regional, and local levels. They maintain links with the Organisation of Honduran Peasants (OCH), which was set up by ex-members of the National Campesino Union. Other *campesino* organisations also set up women's sections, including the National Association of Honduran Peasants (ANACH), with ANAMUC, the National Association of Campesina Women, and the CNTC with its section for women's affairs.

The 1980s saw increasing interest in gender issues. The Sandinista revolution in Nicaragua, the civil wars in El Salvador and Guatemala, and the increasing influence of US politics and military presence in Honduras all served to bring the country's problems of dependency, violence, and corruption to international attention. US military bases brought a rapid increase in the numbers of women and children earning their living through prostitution; HIV and AIDS became serious problems, with Honduras having 60 per cent of Central American cases.[40] Reported rapes and other crimes against women also increased greatly. The first women's organisations focusing specifically on class and gender issues appeared, and research on women's issues began at the university in Tegucigalpa.

In 1984 an urban middle-class women's organisation, the Visitación Padilla (Committee for Peace), was set up, concentrating on women's rights and combating violence against women, with an analysis linking economic exploitation and the position of women. From 1988 it has worked with women's groups in the *barrios* (slums) of Tegucigalpa to encourage their participation in community organisations. Other NGOs began to focus on women's issues, encouraged by a growing interest among donor organisations in funding women's development projects; a number of women's NGOs were also set up towards the end of the

1980s. Many of these are based in Tegucigalpa. The Centre for Women's Studies (CEM) provides a documentation centre and a counselling service for women. The Centre for Women's Rights (CDM, formerly CLADEM-H) trains women on legal issues, among other activities. In 1993 The Association for Popular Development (ADP) opened the first refuge for women in Honduras fleeing domestic violence, in Tegucigalpa.

Categories of women's organisations

Organisations involved with women in a development context in Honduras can be broadly divided into five categories (this is not intended to be an exhaustive list; there are other organisations not mentioned below):

• **Grassroots women's organisations:** these are organisations which exist independently of any union or association. They are few in number, and are found in urban and rural areas.

• **Non-government development organisations (NGDOs):**[41] some of these are women's organisations; others are mixed organisations which have developed policies and programmes for work with women. They vary in character; some are strongly feminist (mixed as well as women's organisations), and committed to political and social change. Others are more instrumentalist, taking a welfare approach, rather than increasing women's capacities to meet their own needs or organise autonomously. Most of them are middle-class organisations, in that they are professionals aiming to provide a service for disadvantaged women, although some employ staff who have become involved in the work through their initial participation as beneficiaries.

• **Popular organisations:** these membership organisations include FEHMUC, CODIMCA and ANAMUC, and the women's sections of the *campesino* unions mentioned above.

• **Institutionalised bodies:** there is a Women's Commission, made up of the women members of the national congress, which has an advisory group that includes representatives from most of the women's NGDOs. Various government departments work with women, including the Ministry of Labour and Social Assistance, the Ministry of Natural Resources (unit for technical co-operation with women and rural youth), the Ministry of Health, and the National Agrarian Institute (INA) with its department of promotion and training of women and rural youth. There is also a women's area within SECPLAN, the secretariat for planning, co-ordination and budget. In most of these institutions the focus is on women as the people responsible for the well-being of the family.[42]

- **Networks:** these are a recent development. The Red de Mujeres de la Zona Norte (Network of Women of the North Zone) consists of various women's groups, organisations and individuals in and around San Pedro Sula and Progreso. It has a feminist philosophy and acts as a co-ordinating and campaigning group. Enlace de Mujeres Rurales Cristianas is a recently-formed network of *campesina* groups. There is also a network of women's organisations and individuals in Tegucigalpa working on the issue of violence against women.

In addition to the Honduran organisations mentioned above, there are also foreign organisations working with women. Some of these channel government aid, such as CARE, which has played a major role in the distribution of US food aid, or USAID, which is perhaps the most influential foreign organisation working with women. USAID has had a Women In Development policy since 1982.[43] For the most part their work with women is within mixed programmes, although recent self-build schools projects, working specifically with women, have been deemed a success by the agency and may lead to more women-only work. Other foreign organisations are mostly independent NGDOs. As with the local NGDOs, their approaches vary considerably. Some are operational, running their own projects and programmes (as was the case with Save the Children (UK) until the early 1990s). Some, like Oxfam UK/I, act primarily as funders, working through local project partners.

For my research project in Honduras, I decided to look at two women's organisations in contrasting areas of Honduras, in order to try to discover the extent to which these groups encouraged or facilitated the empowerment of their members, and how this related both to the specific ways of working with women adopted in the groups, and the external circumstances. In chapter 4 I give an account of a training programme for health promoters, and in chapter 5, an account of Programa Educativo de la Mujer.

4

Case study 1: Health promoters' training programme, Urraco

Urraco: Background

Urraco is in the department of Yoro, north of El Progreso (see Figure 3). It is an agricultural area dominated by the production of bananas (Yoro produces 75 per cent of the Honduran Banana crop)[1] and African palm. There is one small town of 5000 inhabitants, Urraco Pueblo, and the remainder of the population (about 3000 people) lives in scattered villages and hamlets and in the banana camps.

The largest landowner, with between 30 and 50 per cent of the land (some 6000ha), is the Tela Railroad Company, which is actually a big banana company, part of the multinational United Brands. Another 25-30 per cent of land is owned by the co-operatives growing African palm that make up Hondupalma. Of the remainder, about half is owned by cattle farmers and plantain producers; the rest is in the hands of *campesinos* growing maize, plantain, avocado, cassava, and other crops largely for home consumption. Many people have no land — an estimated 10 per cent do not even have a yard for a home garden. The area, therefore, has a number of people in relatively well-paid work, and a majority population of temporary workers and *campesinos*.

The Tela Railroad Company ('the company', as it is known locally) is profoundly influential in the local economy. It arrived in 1895, and is the area's largest employer, both of permanent and casual workers. Men work on the banana plantations and women are employed in the packing plants. Both generally work long hours, though work for women depends on the size of the harvest on a given day, and some days there is none. Work for the company is better paid than other work available locally — men will earn 28 *lempiras* per day as opposed to the 10–12 *lempiras* (about £1 in 1992) for work on a plantain plantation or other day-labouring work; women earn 32–35 *lempiras* for a 12-hour day in the packing plants, for a maximum of three days per week. Permanent workers also receive many benefits in kind, the most significant of which is free housing, to a standard rarely found elsewhere in the sector outside Urraco Pueblo, with running water, sanitation, and electricity, and access to schools, health care, and recreational facilities. Only permanent workers are eligible for these wooden, mostly semi-detached houses on stilts with one room upstairs, one downstairs, and a tiny kitchen and toilet/shower room at the back. There are 12 banana camps in the sector, each housing about 100 workers and their families.

Labour laws in Honduras are quite favourable to permanent employees, who are among other things entitled to receive *prestaciones* — a sum of money and benefits related to length of service — when they leave their job. Given the current economic climate in Honduras, many employers, including Tela, are replacing permanent workers with casual or contract workers. Not only does this remove the job security and fringe benefits, but it also significantly reduces a worker's annual income, as labour laws stipulate that the same person cannot be re-contracted immediately without their becoming eligible for permanent worker benefits. In the past few years, workers have been employed on a 90-day contract and then have a 12-month gap before being re-contracted. Some of the banana camp houses now lie empty.

Most people in Urraco arrived as migrants from other parts of Honduras. They left with the dream of going to the north coast (perceived as where the opportunities are) and maybe to the USA; some having already migrated twice or more within Honduras. Many young people were born in the sector, but according to an ex-official of the banana workers' union, SITRATERCO, none of the over-40s were. The population is almost exclusively *mestizo*; the non-Spanish part of the heritage of people in the area is very diverse. The north coast of Honduras is where the black population of Honduras lives, some of whom came from the British Carribbean. Many people have relatives who have moved to the USA, mostly as illegal immigrants.

Urraco Pueblo

Urraco Pueblo is situated on the railway track about an hour's drive along a dirt road to the north of El Progreso. It acts as a minor commercial centre and focal point, with the sector's only secondary school (only equipped for *plan básico*, the first three years) and a small clinic. The only further education available is sewing classes, which give young women in particular the possibility of obtaining employment in the export processing zones around San Pedro Sula, the second city of Honduras and the industrial, commercial, and financial centre for the north coast. Many young people leave Urraco Pueblo and the surrounding villages in search of work, and never return.

There are several small shops and workshops, and the police have a post in Urraco Pueblo, but for most dealings with the state and to buy any but the most basic items, people have to travel to El Progreso. For education beyond *plan básico* people have to go to El Progreso or San Pedro Sula. There is a regular if crowded bus service between El Progreso and Km. 45, the furthest banana camp, which passes through all the camps and through Urraco Pueblo. There is also a passenger train (the only railways in Honduras were built to serve the banana plantations), leaving El Progreso early in the morning and returning in the early evening, on alternate days. Most people use bicycles — the one-speed Chinese variety — to get to and from work and for transporting loads.

The best housing in Urraco Pueblo is either of breeze block, wood, or adobe with zinc roofs and some concrete floors. The poorer housing is made of *bajareque* (adobe) or plantain leaf spines with thatch roofs and dirt floors. Most houses in the town have electricity and water, either to a tap, or in a well which may have a pump. Most, though not all, houses also have sanitation, either in the form of a WC to a septic tank, or as a pit latrine. The houses vary in size, but rarely have more than a kitchen and one or two other rooms; most have a small yard where chickens and pigs are raised (the pigs also roam the town freely) and where coconut and banana palms and perhaps a few vegetables may grow.

Many households are numerous, with one or two adults and up to 13 children. Some households now use bottled gas or electric stoves, but the great majority still use the traditional wood stove for cooking. Wood is in very short supply and has to be purchased from travelling *leña* (fuelwood) sellers.

As in the rest of Honduras, Urraco sector has a predominantly Catholic population. There is a large Catholic church, which has a church hall and some residential accommodation and which also runs a rehabilitation centre for severely malnourished children. There is, however, a growing interest in the activities of several Protestant sects, five of which have congregations in Urraco Pueblo.

Village life

Life in the villages (there are about 40 of varying sizes) is very different from life in the camps or the town. Villages close to Urraco Pueblo are more likely to have a water supply, usually a well with a pump, and sanitation, usually pit latrines. But further out many people have neither, and rely on water supplies which are often contaminated. In the villages where members of the African palm co-operatives live there are often concrete block housing and tin roofs, but elsewhere almost all the housing is of plantain leaf spines and banana thatch roofs with dirt floors. Many but not all of the villages have primary schools, but it is not unusual for a school to be closed because of a lack of teachers, or to have one teacher teaching five grades. The level of illiteracy in the sector as a whole is about 40 per cent; but in some villages it reaches 90-100 per cent; among older people, women are less literate than men; among younger people the reverse is the case.[2]

The banana camps

There is a big cultural difference between the banana camps and the villages. The camps have a lively atmosphere and are relatively sophisticated. As in Urraco Pueblo, most households have a television and are exposed to outside influences in a way that villagers are not; people have more money, which they often use for luxury consumer goods, clothing, and so on. Young people in the camps dress in the latest fashions, and their posture and voice reflect a confidence and self-awareness not seen elsewhere in the sector. People from the camps are also more mobile, using public transport to visit El Progreso and San Pedro Sula.

Health care

Except in the banana camps, health care provision is poor. The clinic in Urraco Pueblo is poorly-resourced and lacking in medicines; the only other options people have are to go to El Progreso or to use the services of local knowledgeable people. The advent of the health promoter training scheme has made a basic range of pharmaceutical products available, in many of the communities. People's general health is poor; malnutrition is a major problem and contributes to other health problems, although the amount of severe malnutrition among children has been falling. Parasitic infections are frequent because of poor hygiene and poor water quality. Malaria is endemic and dengue is common. Because most houses lack any form of waste water drainage, there are many pools of stagnant water, particularly after heavy rain, perfect for mosquito breeding. Eight cases of cholera were reported in the area in the eight months prior to my visit. Respiratory infections and tuberculosis are common, as well as syphilis (although this is not talked about). It is also likely that there is a hidden incidence of HIV/AIDS infection, given that Honduras has 60 per cent of Central American cases and the north coast is one of the worst-affected areas.[3] If this is so, the problem is going undiagnosed, probably because people die of opportunistic, poverty-related diseases.

Social problems

Honduras, as we have seen in chapter 3, is a country with a strong tradition of *machismo*, and this can be seen very clearly in the level of violence in society. There is much fighting between men and it is not at all uncommon for bodies to be found floating in the River Ulúa. It is said that criminals from other parts of the country come to Urraco to hide. Shots can certainly be heard from time to time. Drunkenness affects as many as 80 per cent of working men, and there is much gambling. There are about 40 bars in Urraco Pueblo (one per 32 adult males), and in the villages there will generally be a bar or someone selling *guaro* (spirits). There is also a growing drug problem among young people, so far, apparently, only involving the use of marijuana, but this has been linked to a rise in robbery over recent years.

Law enforcement is virtually non-existent — certainly justice is beyond the reach of the poorest people. Although the country is now ruled by a civilian government, the military still wield much power, often locally as *caudillos* or *caciques*, 'strong men'. When I interviewed an ex-union leader in his home near one of the banana camps, he told me 'The armed forces are still strong here. We live in relative peace now, but if there was trouble I wouldn't be talking with you — there are spies everywhere. I would be in danger.'

The lives of women in Urraco

The general pattern of activity for women is broadly similar in the camps and in the villages. Their day begins at 4 or 4.30 in the morning, milling corn or taking it to the mill, and ends when they go to bed at 10pm. The migration history of the area means that few women have support from an extended family network. Most women keep a few chickens, and some raise a pig that will usually be sold rather than consumed in the home. Some women take lunch to their husbands at work in the plantations, which may involve a long walk.

Given that there is so little employment available for women, income generation is predominantly home-based. Women will cook food to sell — *tortillas, tamales*, biscuits, anything they might be able to exchange for a few *centavos*. Some make cheese, and some do other people's washing. But all these activities are very limited in scope, as the vast majority of the population are poor. Activities to provide goods for sale in the local market bring low returns and are also very labour-intensive. The labour of older children becomes a significant factor both in caring for younger offspring and also in doing the selling. Many daughters, when they are old enough (14 or 15) leave to go to the *maquila* around San Pedro Sula. This move is seen with mixed feelings. It is a step that leads to (relatively) well-paid employment, at least for a while. But the factories are infamous for exploitative working conditions.

The contraceptive pill is available sometimes in the health centre in Urraco Pueblo, and in pharmacies in El Progresso, but is not easily available for most women. There is also a deep-seated suspicion of it. Female sterilisation is the more common means of controlling fertility, once a woman has a number of children; that, too, requires a visit to El Progresso. In Honduras, it is extremely rare for men to be sterilised.

Very few women are active in any sort of community organisation. A small number of women are members of village water committees, but none are involved in the *patronatos* (village councils). A few women have belonged to housewives' clubs or other groups. Most women active outside the home are involved in the Catholic church, as catechists, or as cleaners and decorators of the church. There is a very small number of (female) *delegadas de la palabra* (delegates of the word; most are male): people trained to lead church services and in other ways compensate for the shortage of priests. Women who work in the *empacadoras* (packing plants) are members of SITRATERCO and may go on training courses and attend meetings.

Domestic violence

A major factor in women's lives in Urraco is domestic violence. It is seen as *'casi lo normal'* (almost the norm);. 'there are men who say that the woman who isn't hit every day won't be free from worries, won't be happy'.[4] Although it is not always physical, 'with just about every couple it exists, they have their problems... sometimes you can hear blows with the flat of a machete blade'.[5] Violence is a factor that not only dominates women's lives but severely limits their choices, as one group of women described to me:

If the woman decides to separate from him, he kills her. He pursues her. If she tries to use the law, he kills her. Some women go to the USA instead, they escape. Some men even follow her there. (Urraco Pueblo Group)

Eva María, a member of the Health Programme co-ordinating team, summed up the kind of life that most women lead in the area in a rather graphic way when I asked her about the situation for women:

*The man takes advantage. If only he is working he says 'I maintain you'.. he
maintains you, but I tell you, it's a life like that of a pig, that he is fattening up,
and at some point he will...* [laughter]. *Women here suffer a lot.* (Eva María, 33)

The Urraco health promotion programme

The health promoters' programme in Urraco was set up in 1985. It was
initiated by a volunteer from the USA who had been placed in the area by
Concern America, a small NGDO, to work alongside the Catholic church
in *promoción feminina* and with the church's child-nutrition centre. It
seems that she found her work there very frustrating: the mothers would
appear from the villages with severely malnourished children, who
would be nursed back to health and returned to their families — but
there was no preventive work being done. So with Concern's support she
set up the health programme to train health promoters to work in the
communities.

The programme took the form of a two-year course, to train members
of the local communities in preventive health care and basic treatments.
About 80 women were recruited to the course, of whom about half
completed the two years. A second recruitment had a similar drop-out
rate. The women participate voluntarily in the course and get a certificate
of completion at the end. The programme has come to have the characteristics of an organisation, with its own financial accounting and division
of labour.

The course is organised around study circles in 26 communities,
including some of the camps, which use the book *Donde No Hay Doctor*
(*Where There is no Doctor*) as a text.[6] The circles meet weekly for about two
hours; there are also monthly sectoral meetings, where all the groups get
together to study a theme, often with an outside speaker. Eighty health
promoters have been trained within a three-and-a-half-year period;
about 100 women were active in the programme at the time of my
fieldwork, 60 as health promoters and 40 in other peripheral activities
such as meals for malnourished children, craft work or goat projects.

The main activity of the health promoters is to carry out a monthly
child-weighing session in their community. Mothers bring children
under five to be weighed, and records are kept of the child's progress.
When the child is underweight, the promoters will talk to the mother
about what she could do to improve the child's nutrition. The results
have been good in terms of reducing the numbers of children suffering
third- or second-degree malnutrition, though it seems there is more
difficulty in reaching and maintaining 'normal' nutritional status.[7]
Attendance at weighing sessions generally started off high but then

dwindled. Some of the promoters put in a lot of time in persuading the mothers to bring their children to the weighing sessions, others do not. The sessions I attended were very varied: many mothers came to some sessions, and thoughtful advice was given to them when they needed it; on other occasions attendance was poor; some children were brought by elder siblings and it seemed unlikely that the advice on nutrition would result in any changes in these cases. At the time, there was a great scarcity of beans, as it was just before the next harvest: the price of beans had increased dramatically and people had little more than *tortillas* and salt to eat. All except one of the children had lost weight that month, and it was clear that information about varying the diet and feeding vegetables was not going to have much impact. However, Padre Chema, the parish priest in charge of the child feeding centre in Urraco Pueblo, was full of praise for the programme and its impact in reducing demand at the feeding centre.

Once the promoters in a community have completed a certain section of the course, they are given a *botiquín* or medicine chest, stocked with 15 basic medicines that they have by then learned to prescribe and administer. One *botiquín* goes to each community, and the promoters take it in turns to house it for a month at a time. People in the community can come to them at any time of the day or night for medical advice and treatment. When she hands the *botiquín* on to the next person, the promoter does an inventory of the contents and accounts are settled. The *botiquínes* are replenished from central supplies maintained by the co-ordinating team, and the medicines are priced to cover purchase and transportation costs but not to make a profit. When necessary the co-ordinators go to San Pedro Sula to buy stocks. The health promoters are unpaid volunteers.

The current Concern volunteer at the time of my research, Monica, has encouraged the women in the programme to make contact with other women's organisations. Some of this networking has been with women's organisations on the north coast: several women go to the meetings of the recently formed Red de Mujeres de la Zona Norte (network of north-zone women) which is a group of women from other *campesina* women's organisations, 'popular organisations', and NGDOs. They have made exchange visits with women working on health issues in other parts of the country. Networking has also taken place at an international level, with members of the co-ordinators' team going to conferences and seminars in the Dominican Republic, Nicaragua, Costa Rica, and Chile.

Concern has been funding the health programme and a literacy programme for about eight years, and is now planning a gradual withdrawal of its financial support.[8] Both programmes are planning fundraising from other sources, and activities to generate income. Because of this, the two programmes, which until recently operated completely separately, have started to strengthen their links and have joint meetings once a month, with the occasional longer 'retreat' together.

Until now the health programme, although officially part of the church's *promoción feminina*, has maintained a semi-autonomous status because of its external funding. This has enabled the organisers to work freely in a way that they could not have done if they had been fully within the church structure. It has not been a conflict-free relationship, but has been reasonably smooth.

The co-ordinating team

The co-ordinating team consists of five women working full time for 450 Lempiras a month (about £45); the team co-ordinator gets a higher wage; there is also one part-time worker. They each have responsibility for three to six of the 26 study circles (though they work in pairs where possible), and they meet with each circle regularly, and also attend the weighing sessions. They supervise the *botiquínes* and generally encourage and motivate women to remain active or to become involved. The sectoral meetings are planned and led by members of the team. The team co-ordinator now produces the regular reports to the funders and keeps the accounts. Previously this latter role was filled by the Concern volunteer, but since deciding to leave she has been gradually handing over her responsibilities and training the team.

The achievements of the Urraco health programme

The programme was not set up with the specific aim of empowering women; but it has recently become an aim of the Concern volunteer and some of the co-ordinating team. The original intention was to meet an urgent practical need of the communities for health care — which is most keenly experienced by women in their roles as mothers.

Personal empowerment

Women, both in the study circles and in the co-ordinating team, emphasised strongly the increase in self-confidence and self-esteem that they had experienced as a result of their participation in the health programme's activities. Members of the study circles talked about losing their shyness and embarrassment. This was described graphically by Mercedes, who lives in a village about half-an-hour's walk outside Urraco Pueblo. Before becoming involved in the programme, her life was heavily restricted:

A:...*I didn't go out, I was too shy to go out.*

Q: *Not even to go to the corner shop?*

A: *No, not alone. Not to go to mill maize or even to run errands, no, I was too shy. [My husband] ran the errands, he said 'if I don't run the errands we won't get to eat'; he brought everything to the house and I didn't go out, until I started to go to Urraco, where we started to get to know each other, to talk about things. It was only with all the lasses there that I started to come awake, to talk. Even in school I was too shy to talk, I didn't like it when I was asked something because I was too embarrassed...*

Q: *So when you started with the programme you still didn't have much confidence?*

A: *No, no. ...*

Q: *And did that change?*

A: *Yes, a lot.*

Q: *What is it like now?*

A: *Even with the women in the group I was too shy to speak, at first. I listened when I arrived; I sat there during the first days... Now it's not like that, we chatter like parakeets when we go there. Now we know each other well.*
(Mercedes, 27)

Rosa, who lives in the Birichiche banana camp, saw similar changes in the women in her group:

There are some who at the beginning hardly said a word. Now that we know each other more, we tell each other with more confidence about the problems we have. This is the biggest change. There were some of us who used to arrive and stay quiet, that's different now. (Rosa, 18)

Laura, from another of the villages, also commented on this change:

Through having meetings, getting to know more people, that's how you lose your shyness and embarrassment, that's how you pick up more confidence and that's how you learn more. (Laura, 38)

Laura also talked about a change in her self-perception relative to other women in her community, but with an interestingly mixed attitude:

Now I feel different... Sometimes a neighbour will come in the night with a child who feels sick and I know which medicine to give her to get rid of the illness. So now I feel better than her...You learn things in order to share them. If you learn and turn selfish, only using it for yourself, you're not doing anything. (Ibid.)

The increase in self-confidence was a factor in my ability to obtain interviews, as Mercedes pointed out:

I have changed a lot, and I can tell you now, talking to you like this, without shyness, or talking to a neighbour, asking her things, discussing things ... before I would have been too shy. I could have been in pain, but I wouldn't tell anyone except [my husband]. (Mercedes, 27)

Another aspect of personal empowerment highlighted by the women I interviewed was the learning of new skills. These included diagnosing common medical conditions and treating them, taking temperatures, and giving injections, keeping track of children's nutritional status through weighing sessions, and so on. The women talk with great satisfaction of having learned these skills. Laura again:

I was happy to learn about things I didn't know, because around here we don't know about remedies ... about simple medicines for the children. If a child gets a temperature what you do is wrap it up warmly, even though that bakes the child. Through these studies I've learned now about how to treat a child if it is ill. It's better to undress it and use damp cloths to lower the fever. They used to say not even to wash the child. But if the child is burning up it's better to put cool things on it. It's a joy to learn these things that I didn't know before. (Laura, 38)

Weighing children regularly has been a major activity of the programme. To begin with, the women in the groups were not confident:

...the first few times it was hard to learn the weighing, you had to learn to use the scales, how to fill in the record card, how to explain it to the mother. A lot of times [Dolores] *showed us and we didn't understand anything. She came there to help us, 'look at this, you have to do this and that', that's how we learned, fearfully, we filled in the card, 'that's right' she'd say, and that's how we gradually learned.* (Mercedes, 27)

The weighing sessions that I observed all had a member of the coordinating team present and playing a central role.

For some women, the learning of new skills enabled them to obtain employment, or to get involved in other projects. Iginia, who had left the programme because it could not offer her a salary, had joined a local committee working on the provision of a hospital in Urraco Pueblo which was in the early stages of construction while I was there. She was optimistic about her chance of obtaining a job as a result of her involvement. The number of women who could get jobs using their new skills in this way was, however, very limited, especially since the health promoter training is nowhere near as comprehensive as nursing training, and opportunities are scarce. Three of the 120 women who have passed through the programme have been successful in getting jobs that use the skills learned on the programme. It is interesting that some women who have left the programme have done so because they feel they should be paid to do the work of a health promoter:

We have encountered serious problems, because now the promoters think, with the little bit of training we have given them, that they can aspire to other things, so they are asking us for a salary, for us to pay them, and how on earth can we pay them? (Marcela, 40, co-ordinating team)

It takes at least a minimum sense of self-worth and self-confidence for someone to state that their time and effort is worth payment, and to set conditions on their involvement.

In focusing on women's rights, the programme has helped some women change their self-image, and increase their sense of self-esteem. Rosa illustrates this in her description of the man she wants to marry:

It'll be difficult, but when I marry I'd like my husband to be like this: that he shares the work with me. Men have a right to help in the kitchen too, to wash the dishes, to sweep, in complete democracy. Often the women will be washing and the man arrives tired from work, he arrives demanding 'bring me my food' and she has to leave off washing to give food to him and the children. But he should be able to see that she is doing the washing and instead to serve the food, to fetch the tortillas... Everything should be shared, including the washing up. (Rosa, 18)

Monica, the Concern volunteer, gave me her view of the changes experienced by women through participating in the Programme:

...women are more independent, more confident... They're more willing to speak up, they're more willing to leave, they go on courses when their husbands aren't in agreement... Whereas before they wouldn't have gone at all.

The effects of the programme on personal empowerment are far more marked in the women who are members of the co-ordinating team than in the general groups. Some of them moved into the team after being in the groups, and team membership has given them many more opportunities to move out of their traditional position within the home and into the wider world. In some cases this has included moving out into the international arena, through attending training courses and conferences in other countries. Dolores, the team leader, who started her involvement as a trainee health promoter in a study circle, talks about travelling outside the local community:

I'd never been to Tegucigalpa. I went the first time with Monica and then alone. And I've been to La Paz, via Comayagua. I went on my own, asking for directions, scared. You find your way. (Dolores, 28, co-ordinating team)

She also describes her first visit abroad:

I had never imagined that I would go to another country. I went to the Dominican Republic the year before last. It was good. It was a course on natural medicines. When Monica suggested it I told her I didn't want to go, I was afraid, of going alone — the airport, going through Miami — afraid that I'd lose myself. I spent a month thinking about it. But I enjoyed it. I've received various letters from friends I made there. I learned a lot too. ... And now I've been to Costa Rica and Chile. I think about the fact that I'm going to learn and later be able to share it with people. (Ibid.)

For Juana, currently working as a part-time member of the co-ordinating team, participation in the programme has changed her irreversibly:

It's where my critical consciousness started. I started to know about my reality as a woman and what women need... I already had quite a bit of confidence because of my work in the church. I had awareness... I've changed a lot, because before I was a very introverted woman because of being a single mother. People reject you, you're alone with a daughter.. I've always been sensitive to the criticism. The programme has helped me a lot. I have discovered for myself that I am worth something, even if I am a single mother. I know that I can achieve my goals; that I like to fight.

Q: *And are there things you do now that you wouldn't have done before?*

A: *I go out. I go out freely, and now I'm not as bothered by what people say. I have more communication with people, I have more faith in sharing more with other women... I will defend myself now.* (Juana, 37)

Monica described changes she had seen in the co-ordinating team members during her time working with them. She noted the increase in levels of confidence, and observed that this was not only visible in familiar settings, but elsewhere too:

[You can see they are] more confident, the way they hold themselves. And both within the community and outside, daring to go to more professional settings and feel more comfortable, like with the banks. Knowing how to send a fax, or even knowing what a fax is. (Monica)

Empowerment in relationships

Some women connected with the health programme have made changes in their relationships with their husbands and families:

[My husband] and I understand each other better now. ...We say things to each other. We share things that he wants to share with me, like money, we decide what we will spend it on, what we will buy, all that, and sometimes we don't even have to talk about it, about what we're going to eat... because we know what each other's likes are, we get on well together. (Mercedes, 27)

She later explains that he shares some of the childcare now:

Now if he has to go out to a meeting I stay at home, [and if I have to go out,] he stays at home to look after the girls. (Ibid.)

Reina, one of the co-ordinating team, describes changes she has gone through:

Before ... I didn't value myself; rather I was subject to the man. My first husband treated me badly. He told me 'you are no use as a wife'; and what I did was start crying, and he would say 'I'm going to look for another wife better than you'. Now it's not like that. Now I know that we're equal, that all women are equal, and with him, well... I'm not going to die over all that. Now I claim my rights, and I've done all sorts of things. (Reina, 31, co-ordinating team)

Changes are not only in relationships with husbands. Reina goes on to talk about her relationship with her children:

Before, with my children, I would hit them and get hysterical with them and all that. Now I don't do that. I treat my children with love. I don't go around hitting them, I care for them. Who else is going to care for them for me? Before I used to hit them with a belt like a madwoman, when I just lived shut in the house. If my mother says to me 'the kids did such and such, you should hit them for it, you haven't hit them', I say 'no, if I don't care for my children, who will?' (Ibid.)

Padre Chema, the local Catholic priest, told me that he had noticed changes in the relationships within the families of some women in the programme:

I couldn't generalise much, but in the families that I know, I have seen that ... the family is changing a bit. The woman participates now. The fact that they think about family problems and the abuses they experience, well, it gives them the capacity to put forward their own points of view... So a woman who talks about her difficulties, on a personal level, with more sureness and more critical capacity, I think she's the one that makes the man enter more into dialogue. You can see that the atmosphere within the family has changed a little. (Padre Chema)

Again, the most marked changes in close relationships can be seen in members of the co-ordinating team. They move around among the communities, and the women have had to make the changes in their personal situations necessary to enable and sustain such freedom of movement. In Dolores' case, her life has almost certainly taken a very different form because of her participation in the programme. When I asked her what had changed because of being in the programme, she told me:

I've learned ... to think twice before getting married. You have to think carefully about it. I think you have to train the man who'll be your husband well, so that when you get married you understand him. Perhaps if I hadn't got into the programme I would have got married, but I've had so much training, about the attitude the man should have towards women ... that you shouldn't have children without planning and wanting them.. Perhaps I'd be married with a pile of children. I'm not in a hurry. Everything in its time. I'll get married when I want to. Not when someone requires it of me. We'd have to be in agreement, and if one doesn't want to then we won't. (Dolores, 28)

Eva María, the longest-serving member of the co-ordinating team, has noticed significant, though limited, changes in her relationship with her husband:

Before it was more him who made the money decisions, but little by little... it's changed quite a bit. Now there's been some progress in relation to all that, to domination. ... it's been about a year, and I've been working for five years. It's not in everything, though... (Eva María, 33)

Collective empowerment

My interviews with women in the study circles did not provide much evidence of collective empowerment. Some activities were being undertaken as a group, but this did not result in the groups becoming more able to organise collectively to meet their needs or gain more access to economic, social or political power. Much of this was to do with the way in which the programme was structured, and in particular its 'course' structure.

The Birichiche group provides an example of the kind of group activities that were undertaken. The women organised a small-scale 'credit union' (as they called it), where each woman regularly saved one lempira per month. The joint savings were later used to provide each woman with a uniform for the programme's graduation ceremony (*clausura*). This no doubt made an important contribution to their sense of belonging and identity, but falls far short of making a significant contribution to their ability to take charge of their lives. Another group activity which was undertaken for the monthly sectoral meetings was the preparation of role plays.

The co-ordinating team, however, did show evidence of collective empowerment. Having in the past been run more or less entirely by the previous US volunteer, the programme was now almost entirely being managed and run by the team. They were all involved, although most responsibility rested on Dolores as the team co-ordinator. Dolores was of the opinion that, if the previous volunteer had not been replaced, the programme would have folded at that point, but that the replacement volunteer had worked to ensure the programme could be sustained by the co-ordinating team when she left:

Monica has done a lot. She has given us follow-up support. If she hadn't come the programme would probably have collapsed. People were used to having someone from outside the country... Above all she's given us confidence, because she's handed over the management of the books to us, which we didn't have the opportunity to do before; the accounts, the buying and selling of our medicines...

Q: *And did she show you how to do them?*

A: *Yes, especially me, because I've been the person closest to her. We worked on the reports together... She's encouraged us a lot.*

Q: *And what will happen when she goes?*

A: *The programme will be in our hands.*

Q: *And what will that be like?*

A: *...We're confident of succeeding. We're hoping the programme will continue.* (Dolores, 28, co-ordinating team)

Members of the co-ordinating team are also involved in networking activities, including exchanges with organisations in other parts of the country, participation in the Red de Mujeres de la Zona Norte, the feminist meetings and Enlace de Mujeres Cristianas Rurales, the Rural Christian Women's Network (a small number of the women from the study circles are also involved directly in these groups). They are known to other women's organisations, though this is perhaps more as individuals than as an organisation *per se*.

There is no doubt in the minds of local people that the health programme has had a positive impact on child nutrition in the zone. This, however, does not mean that the programme has created opportunities for women to work together on activities that will enable them to take charge of their situations or act powerfully as a group to influence other aspects of their lives.

The story of Nelly Suazo

A recent event has put the programme participants and the co-ordinating team under great stress. This was the brutal murder of one of the most active study circle co-ordinators, Nelly Suazo.

In 1991, Nelly Suazo joined the Urraco health promoters' training programme. She arrived at the programme 'a *mujer aplastada* — over whelmed, crushed, without enthusiasm, discouraged, tired, squashed'. She was the fifth of thirteen children, one of seven who survived. Her childhood was marked by poverty, and abuse from her father, who drank away his banana-plantation wages. As the eldest surviving daughter, she worked hard in the home, helping her mother raise her siblings, and she left school after third grade to earn money selling whatever her mother could put together. At 17 she moved into her boyfriend's parents' house, where she was responsible for domestic work. Later she and her boyfriend moved into their own house. He started being violent with her before the birth of their first child. Over the years it got worse, though Nelly never complained to others.

It was after the fourth baby was born — the girl died at six months — that she joined the programme. At first Nelly would sit quietly. Gradually she began to open up and get involved. Then her husband began to object to her participation; he finally violently threatened to abandon the family if she did not give up her involvement. Something snapped inside her and she told him to go. Nelly continued with the programme, increasing her involvement. She became well-known for her creativity and her love of sociodrama, through which she, with other women, expressed insights into their lives, often raising the issue of domestic violence.

Nelly became involved in the Red de Mujeres de la Zona Norte, meeting with women from other parts of the country; once she excitedly travelled to Tegucigalpa as a delegate to a national women's meeting, and was radiant with the impact of the visit for weeks afterwards.

During this time her sister Glenda had become involved with a man who was treating her badly. Nelly actively supported her and encouraged her to leave him, which she did. Then on 8 April 1993, — Holy Thursday — Glenda received a message from her ex-partner telling her to come to his house to collect some money from him. Suspicious, Glenda took Nelly with her. The man was not in when they arrived in the early evening. It was late, and they took a short-cut home though the banana plantation. They walked into a trap. The man and a friend were waiting for them with machetes. Nelly was brutally murdered and Glenda was left for dead. They were found 17 hours later, hidden under banana leaves.

Nelly's murder was a profound shock for the health promoters' programme and for the entire community; it took on a particular significance, the news coming as it did on Good Friday. At first there was shock and numbness. Then despair. Some women talked of abandoning the programme. Then some people got angry, and the fight to get the murder dealt with by the legal process provided a focus for action. Within the Honduran legal system it is very hard for poor people to get justice, and even reporting the murder took a month of bureauratic to-ing and fro-ing. And this with the murderers known, and living in the community.

Eventually, the community took matters into its own hands: one of the men was 'captured' by friends and members of Nelly's family and he was delivered to the authorities and imprisoned; but Glenda's ex-partner was still at large in September 1993.

Several people told me of feeling as if there was no point in continuing the work, soon after the tragedy happened. However, as time passed, Nelly's murder, and the subsequent efforts to obtain justice and to support her family, had the effect of gathering women together and making them more determined to continue. It gave them something to react against and organise about. The second Honduran Feminist Gathering was named in memory of Nelly Suazo, and the Urraco women saw their concern being taken up in a national arena. Although it provided a focus for organising, it did not push the women to develop strategising and planning skills, to confront a powerful institution within their own communities or to have to defend their own programme and assert their commitment to it and belief in it. They were able, however, to move from seeing Nelly's case as an illustration of what happens to women who step out of line, to an example of a woman who had taken on great challenges, who must be remembered with pride, and who provides inspiration to those that remain to continue to push for equality and justice.

An analysis of empowerment in the Urraco health programme

It is clear that some empowerment has taken place, but that this has been predominantly limited to personal empowerment. What enabled a process of empowerment to take place and what inhibited it?

Aspects working in favour of the empowerment process

Particular individuals have played significant roles in the development of the programme and therefore of any empowerment that has taken place within it, although no single individual has provided a strong driving force throughout. The programme was initiated by a US volunteer with CONCERN, Katherine Burke, who was a nutritionist. Her organising and encouragement and the efforts of Eva María, one of the first co-ordinators, helped the initial establishment of the study circles. Monica, the next US volunteer, was more of a general organiser. She encouraged the co-ordinating team to take more responsibility for the content of the programme, while she concentrated on the organisational aspects. It is significant that Monica had a strong personal commitment to women's empowerment. So although the programme did not have specific goals of empowering women, she was thinking about ways to help the process of empowerment take place, and how to structure activities to facilitate it:

My goal in my own mind has been to see the women blossom, to use a qualitative statement. To see them come to life, to find the life in themselves, whether that be as a health promoter or whatever... To be able to have hope, for their own lives, for their communities, to feel animated... (Monica)

It was through her initiative that the themes covered in the sectoral meetings were widened out from issues related directly to health to broader issues, for example, treating violence against women as a health issue. She was clear that for personal empowerment to happen in the study circles, it needed to be happening within the co-ordinating team:

...the team spirit has changed a lot. We've worked through a lot of problems at the beginning; definite conflicts; personality conflicts. I hated the meetings when I first came, because of the tension amongst members, lack of respect, insults, mistrust, it was horrible... I really have worked on that as a goal. In meetings, in allowing them to talk about their personal lives, at first I thought we were really getting off the topic. And then I thought, 'wait a second, this is what it's about'. So that's been really good. I thought that if it really doesn't happen in the team it's not going to happen in the circles either. So that's changed the spirit a lot, sharing our personal lives. (Ibid.)

She was also very supportive of the team's taking on new activities, such as travelling abroad, and latterly, taking over responsibility for the management of the programme's affairs.

The individuals making up the co-ordinating team have also been important in encouraging the women in the study circles. They are all 'local' women (whilst sharing the history of in-migration of large numbers of the local population). Several of them, including the co-ordinator of the team, Dolores, came into their role in the co-ordinating team through the study circles, and thus provide a model to the other women of what can be achieved by women like them. None of them has the charisma which might be expected of leaders in some organisations, which means not only that they have not had to contend with the strong feelings of opposition that charisma seems to generate, but also that what they have achieved has been through dint of hard work and commitment.

Another important individual has been the Catholic Priest, Padre Chema. He came to the area around the time that Monica arrived. He has given support and encouragement in many ways, including providing premises for the sectoral and team meetings, and using his role as priest to reinforce certain aspects of the programme, for example insisting that women have a right to respect and equality. Monica gave me an example of this :

The women say that they really enjoyed learning about health, and they mentioned the women's rights stuff, that this was a whole new thing that they were exposed to and that they were discussing now, it was a topic that's legitimate. And I think it really helps that they see the priest supportive of that. At the clausura (graduation ceremony) he gave a speech on machismo as a grave pecado (sin). (Ibid.)

The programme received support from CONCERN, in the form of the volunteers and the funding for the programme's activities, without which it is unlikely to have developed. There was some support from other external sources as well, in the form of visitors, some of whom then raised funds to contribute to activities. A visit from a women's group in New England, which had heard about the programme through Monica, was referred to several times as an event of great significance, and contact had been maintained through letters and exchange of photographs. Not only did it bring a form of recognition and validation to the work of the programme, but it also appeared to be a factor in changing the sense of isolation and insignificance felt by the Urraco women. By the time I visited them, they no longer needed such external validation, as they were providing their own; but in order to reach the point of being able to validate themselves, some mechanism for challenging the cultural pattern of self-invalidation and sense of worthlessness had been necessary. Other forms of networking and of maintaining contact with current debates, in particular with various national and international women's organisations, also contributed to the process.[9]

The methodology used in the health programme was not particularly innovatory, but some aspects of it nonetheless contributed to the process of personal empowerment experienced by the health promoters. The main 'building block' of the programme was the study circle, a small group of three to fifteen women. This provided a base group within which each woman could build her confidence and take the risks involved in becoming more participative and active. The structure of sectoral meetings provided a forum for a wider exchange, the opportunity to meet more people, participate on a larger scale, and undertake different activities. Sectoral meetings also served the purpose of giving a woman an identity as a member of the whole programme and not just her particular group. Within the sectoral meetings, the use of sociodrama was important. Women in the circles would prepare a role-play on a particular theme. Sometimes these provided the opportunity for the expression of strong emotions, particularly when they related to areas of personal difficulty for the women. Monica again, speaking of changes she has noticed in the women since she first arrived in Urraco:

They've also been more active in presenting sociodramas. Some of the sociodramas just knock my socks off — how explicit they were about the violence at home. Maybe they didn't see a lot of hope for getting out of it in some of the sociodramas, but that they had the awareness and were willing to present that publicly.... And some of the women who presented it were themselves in a situation of violence, and people in the audience knew. And they knew that others knew. But it was like a therapy. We had visitors, and afterwards the visitors were stunned by the obstacles that these women live with and they asked 'what do you do to deal with this, how do you survive?' And Margarita looked at them and laughed and said 'we do sociodramas. That's the way we release our tension.' (Ibid.)

Women in the circles thus had the opportunity to move out of the home and immediate family both physically and psychologically, into a small group and then into a larger group; and some of them took the further step of participating in activities such as the *Red de Mujeres de la zona norte* which gave them an identity and entrance into the wider world.

Another way in which the programme structure encouraged the process of personal empowerment was through the teaching of specific skills. For a very few women, the skills led directly to employment and therefore to a widening of economic choices. For others, learning the skills and using them with members of the local community gave them a sense of self-worth that had been missing before. Their standing in the local community and with their husbands and other members of their families increased. (It would require further research to find out if this effect was lasting for women who left the programme.) I would surmise that, having once learned one set of new skills, a woman would be left with a greater sense of her capacity to learn and take on new activities and of having more ability to take opportunities should they arise. The women who left the programme because they were not being paid as promoters had developed a sense of their self-worth, although they expressed it negatively in terms of the programme.

The Health Programme has a status of semi-autonomy in relation to the Catholic Church structures. It operates under the wing of Promoción Femenina, the church organisation in the region focusing on women, but because it is separately funded, it has a degree of independence, which has perhaps contributed to the development of empowerment, particularly among the co-ordinating team. Some of the activities they have undertaken, such as their participation in Enlace de Mujeres Cristianas Rurales and the Red de Mujeres de la Zona Norte are not approved of by

Promoción Femenina. The team were determined to maintain their independence even after the withdrawal of CONCERN funding.

The leadership style of the programme has been another factor that has encouraged the empowerment process. Co-ordinating team members have been appointed from within the programme, having developed their leadership skills within the study circles. Although the programme was heavily dependent on the foreign volunteers for several years, leadership and control of the programme has apparently successfully been handed over to the local women. A similar process has happened in the literacy programme set up by CONCERN volunteers. However, there are certain aspects of leadership style which could be seen as inhibiting empowerment.

Aspects working against the empowerment process

The chief obstacle to empowerment is the way that the programme has been structured around a two-year training course. This has meant that women have come into the programme with the expectations of learning a set of skills via a finite involvement as 'receivers' of what the course has to offer. Although the actual learning of the skills is a positive factor, the limited expectations have served to minimise the impact in terms of empowerment. Participants have not taken on a sense of full 'ownership' of the programme as theirs to use and develop. They have followed a line of study and action identified by others as relevant to their needs or the needs of the community, seeing participation as a specific means to a limited end. It is significant that, although several of the women identified the desire to serve their community as their motivation for joining the programme, so many left after the graduation ceremony; and the feeling that promoters should be paid for their work was so strong. Such a demand is not unreasonable, but indicates that the programme in and of itself apparently did not meet enough needs for the women to choose to continue to invest their time and energy in it. To provide a forum for the empowerment process, the programme would need to have a structure, focus, and methodology that would motivate women to continue to be active participants, and to use their own initiative to tackle issues which they themselves had identified. However, to encourage a sense of agency in this way might entail a challenge to the programme's semi-autonomous status.

Having health as a main focus of activity may not give sufficient scope for empowerment processes to operate. Health-care problems are a major drain on women's physical, mental, and financial resources, and the provision of affordable health care and the reduction of child malnutrition make women's lives easier. But women are not led to challenge the social, political, and economic relationships which underpin the position of women as main consumers (or would-be consumers) of health provision.

In focusing on training health promoters, the programme has chosen a structure and content that limits the numbers of women who can reasonably participate, since not many women in each community will want to take on that role, and those who do will be the relatively more confident women. In addition, the programme faces a major challenge with regard to funding. The promoters have to charge for medicines, but there is no likelihood of the programme being able to meet its costs through these charges. Without funding, (which is now being gradually withdrawn) it is hard to imagine how the programme will be able to sustain itself, despite the best intentions of the co-ordinating teams of both the health and literacy programmes.

The methodology adopted in the study circles has also limited the empowerment process. The main method for teaching health promoters in the study circles was to work through the book *Donde No Hay Doctor*. The book was produced in response to exactly the kind of circumstances prevailing in Urraco, and its contents are perfectly suitable. At each meeting of the study circles, the women would read a passage once or more and use that as the basis for discussion. This gave them a valuable chance to practise their literacy skills, but limited their opportunities to develop their own themes and agendas. The circles appeared to be very dependent on the co-ordinating team members. Monica confirmed this when I asked her about it:

The co-ordinators always say 'go ahead and run the meeting' but they don't always do it because ... it's like a class. Some circles are better than others, but there's always a strain on the co-ordinators' time; they have outside meetings, outside trainings. It's been easier in the communities where there's been somebody like Rosa working, who's one of the four who was really getting trained as a leader. Rosa would run the meeting, or Juana would run the meeting. So if we have a really strong woman she could go ahead and do it. You should be able to depend on any one of them. (Monica)

The reading of the text is supplemented with practising methods, when relevant, and by sociodramas and sharing of experience. The methodology has reinforced an attitude of dependency and an expectation of solutions coming from the outside, and has not created many opportunities for women to learn from their own mistakes. The expression of strong emotions within the programme were almost all (with the exception of events surrounding the murder of Nelly Suazo), connected with clashes between group members that ended with one or more people leaving the programme.

Although leaders are elected from within the circles to act as circle co-ordinators, the methodology does not encourage those leaders as a group to develop their skills. Some of them have done so, but this seems to be because of their personalities and existing self-confidence rather than through any deliberate training and development within the programme itself. They were not in turn encouraged to foster the development of leadership skills among other members of their groups. In Rosa's case, having been elected to co-ordinate the circle, she became the only person taking responsibility for group activities. If anything needed leadership, she was the one to do it, taking on the role of treasurer and organiser of their 'credit union' as well. That boosted her self-confidence because of her group's confidence in her, but also limited the opportunities for personal development for other members. The co-ordinating team received leadership training from Monica, but it remains to be seen how effective that will be in terms of the programme's continuing functioning.

Cultural and local conditions have also played a part in limiting the process of empowerment in the Urraco Health Programme. Some are similar to those faced elsewhere in the country, including the strength of *machismo* and *caudillismo*. Others are more locally specific. In particular, many of the local communities in the Urraco sector are not well-established because of the strong pattern of in-migration over the past ten years or so. The local culture includes a strong violent element which affects women's lives and their ability to react, respond or take action for themselves. It is possible, too, that the employment-oriented nature of the area, particularly for the women in the camps, and the lack of land available for self-provisioning agriculture, means that women have great difficulty in becoming and staying involved in a programme that requires a regular, inflexible commitment from them.

5

Case Study 2: Programa Educativo de la Mujer, Santa Bárbara

Macuelizo: Background

The parish of Macuelizo where PAEM is located (see Figure 3), lies in the north of the Department of Santa Bárbara, in north-western Honduras. It covers two municipalities, Azacualpa and Macuelizo, both of which are on the western border with Guatemala. The parish includes mountains to the west and north, and part of the Quimistán valley, a fertile plain, running north-eastward towards the coast. The town of Macuelizo is in the north of the municipality of the same name, with a population of 2,456. Azacualpa town, somewhat smaller, is some five miles further north, on a good dirt road. These are the only large concentrations of population in the parish; the rest of the two municipalities' combined population of 45,967 lives in 48 *aldeas* (villages) and 212 *caseríos* (hamlets) scattered across the mountains and the plain.[1] It is one of the most densely populated areas in the department of Santa Bárbara.

The area is agricultural. The varied geography and climate allow a wide range of crops. In the mountains the predominant crops are maize and beans, grown on tiny plots of land (*minifundios*) sometimes owned by small farmers or by co-operatives, but often rented or squatted. Where conditions allow, coffee is cultivated for the market. Lower down the mountains and on the plain other crops can be grown, such as tomatoes, peppers, and chilies. On the plain, where the climate is drier and land is fertile and of good agricultural quality, most land is in the hands of large farmers (*latifundistas*).[2] The predominant crops are sugar cane and rice, and cultivation and processing is dominated by one big company, Chimbagua. There are also tobacco plantations, and cattle ranches; the amount of land under pasture has increased dramatically in the past 30 years. The one main road runs through the Quimistán valley, linking San Pedro Sula, the second city and industrial centre of Honduras, with Santa Rosa de Copán, the Guatemalan border, and the tourist attraction of the Copán ruins. Macuelizo town is about five miles north of the paved road.

Most men in the parish are agricultural workers, either on an own-account basis or as day-labourers for the larger farmers and for Chimbagua. Trucks collect and deposit workers at the start and finish of the day. The large farms have some mechanisation, but most of the work is hard physical labour with a machete. Employment for women is scarce, except during the period of the coffee harvest, and many young women migrate to the Sula valley to work in the *maquila* (assembly plants). Many people currently living in the parish are in-migrants from further west or south, having moved in search of land rather than employment.

Most villages in the parish now have a primary school, and there is a secondary school in each of the municipal centres (a prerequisite for municipality status) and one small agricultural college. Access to primary education is not universal: many of the *caseríos* are long distances from the villages with difficult paths, which become impassable during wet weather. In the mountains the levels of poverty are such that many families do not send children to school, or only do so for a short time, because of the cost of uniforms and materials and the need for the children's labour. A small number of villages now have electricity; a larger number have potable water supplies. But within those villages there are many people without water or electricity, and supply is inconsistent, with power cuts and water cuts.

Most houses in the area are made of adobe, *bajareque* (a kind of wattle and daub) or wood, with dirt floors. Few have more than one or two rooms and perhaps a separate kitchen. Roofs are thatched, or of tile or zinc (the latter being much cheaper). Most households in the villages closer to the roads have pit latrines or, sometimes, septic tanks; more isolated hamlets and villages make do without them. Cooking is on wood stoves; at least one village has organised to have a 'wood lot' to supply the fuel needs of the community, but generally wood is in short supply, and deforestation a growing problem.

The parish has five health centres, including one in each of the towns. Outside the towns formal health care is very poor; health centres are under-staffed and under-resourced, and likely to have medicines for only a few days each month. Women did not expect to receive treatment at a health centre: they expected to be told there was no medicine, or to find the centre closed, or to be ignored. If they can afford it (which few can), people can consult private doctors in La Entrada, about half an hour by bus to the west, and attend hospitals in Santa Rosa de Copán or San Pedro Sula. For the more isolated communities, health care is much less accessible, with walks of six to eight hours, perhaps carrying the sick, in order to reach the paved road. Most communities have a midwife, though not necessarily with formal training or practising modern hygiene. Malnutrition and the diseases of poverty are the main health problems; problems with alcoholism and violence seem to be present in some communities and not so much in evidence in others. There are high levels of illiteracy; few women achieve more than two or three years in primary school.

Many households in the villages and small settlements now have radios; there are some televisions in the towns, but in the villages they are rare — maybe one or two in a village; they pull the crowds for football matches for a small fee. Generally, urban culture is absent, although young people are perhaps now beginning to be influenced by older siblings who have moved away. The culture of *machismo* is very strong.

This part of Honduras is firmly Catholic in religion, although some of the protestant churches are represented, including the pentecostalists.

The experience of women in Macuelizo

The lives of women in the parish of Macuelizo are bounded by the expectations of a clear sexual division of labour, and scanty social services. Their dominant roles are as housewives and mothers, and as carers for small livestock; in some cases women work in agriculture.[3] In the bigger villages there are now mills, either privately or collectively owned, where the soaked maize for *tortillas* can be ground; in smaller settlements this is still done manually using a grinding stone or a simple hand-mill.

Girls now receive more formal education than was usual even as recently as a decade ago. That the main villages now have schools is one factor; another is that the attitude towards girls and education is slowly changing. However, many fathers still do not want their daughters to be educated, seeing it as an encouragement to go out of the domestic sphere. In addition, few girls have mothers who were educated, and there is therefore an absence of a strong role model that would help girls (and their mothers) exert pressure on the issue.

It is unusual for a woman to continue to live in her house after the death or desertion of her *compañero*.[4] She usually moves in with a married child or back with her parents, or leaves for the city. There are few options for her, as the only paid work for women is seasonal labour in the coffee harvest. There are few other ways of earning a living; other than in the towns, people have very little cash, so the possibilities of selling *tamales* or doing washing and so on are limited. A few women travel the mountains with bags of second-hand clothing (shipped in from the US) to sell. It is a relatively lucrative occupation but there is a limited market and a woman has be able to be away from home for days at a time.

Men are generally very vigilant and strict about what women may do. Sonia, now aged 34, told me of being locked into her windowless house when her *compañero* left for the *milpa* in the morning and staying there all day every day until he returned in the late afternoon. She was then in a *unión libre* and 16 or 17 years old. She recounted it as an extreme form of something quite normal. When the man comes home there is another meal to prepare. Some women have other members of their extended family living in the same or next village, and are able to visit or share tasks. Many others do not, having migrated from further afield. Women are generally very isolated from each other, and may not know their own neighbours or the wider community. This varies from one community to another and is linked closely with the lack of any history of organisation, campaigning or church activity.

Some parts of the parish have seen many attempts at organising people. The Catholic Church, through CARITAS, has organised a large number of women's groups over the past 25 years. A few other NGDOs that work with women have done the same more recently. Such groups have usually been involved in administering donations of food or seed, activities such as growing vegetables, and giving information on nutrition and child care. Generally, as soon as the donations stop, the groups collapse. The other main organisers have been the *campesino* organisations such as the CNTC. Most of the CNTC's work has been with the men, but they have also worked with women's groups in some communities. In some parts of the parish, PLAN Honduras, a branch of the big US-based aid agency Foster Plan International, has been very active. It is not common for women to be active members of the *patronato* (village council) or other formal community organisations, although women are active members of base community church groups where they exist.

PAEM: a brief history

PAEM, the Programa Educativo de la Mujer (Women's Educational Programme) was set up in the parish of Macuelizo in 1986. It grew out of the work and vision of María Esther Ruiz, a *campesina* woman who had had opportunities for education and experience beyond those normally available to a poor rural woman. For a long time she planned to become a nun. The local priest made sure she received primary education, and she became an activist, working as a CARITAS promoter with women's groups; as the only woman leader with the ACPH Radio Schools (Honduran Association for Popular Culture); and as the only woman leader in two co-operative federations. Later, she worked for the CNTC, where part of her work involved being on the three-person committee responsible for formulating policy and strategy.

All these experiences left her feeling that there had to be some other way of working with women that did not reproduce conditions of dependency. PAEM was the result. A new priest, Padre Jesús María Aechu, a Basque Passionist in his early thirties, had come to the parish in 1978. He had decided to revitalise Catholic Church activities by having a 'mission' in 1981, spending a week in each village with programmes of activities centred on the church. He asked María Esther to work with women during the mission, and from that work ten initial groups were set up which formed the basis of PAEM. The idea was to build a programme very deliberately from the bottom up, with women identifying their own needs, and working out a response to those needs. María Esther knew the approach she wanted the programme to take:

I had no right to give it a name, or start an NGO, or have an organisation with one, two, three groups. I hadn't the right; nor had two or three of us... We were going to do it together with the women who got involved. The conclusion that I, at least, had come to was that all the work is done from the top down; it was this verticalism that I didn't like, I didn't think things worked that way; we needed to build from the base, which implied more time, more dedication, which is slow work. I thought that was where I had to start.

They remained as a loose association of groups of women who met regularly to share their experiences. By 1985 they felt ready to have a more specific identity — in part to help them in communicating with groups meeting in other parishes. They chose a name which described their work.

PAEM grew significantly. At this time Oxfam UK/I had a Deputy Regional Representative for Mexico and Central America, Deborah Eade, with specific responsibility for their Honduras programme, who was seeking to support work that incorporated a gender dimension, which its existing programme with rural workers' organisations, trades unions, and various intermediary NGOs, did not. She was also looking for work that was outside the factionalism so common in Honduras. She met María Esther and discussed the work in Macuelizo, and recommended that Oxfam should provide funding for this new, unconventional programme, which had clear aims but lacked the explicit targets and objectives usually required by donor agencies. This funding covered the travel and other costs of several part-time co-ordinators, enabling them to work more intensively. The number of groups increased; at one time there were 110 groups in four departments, Santa Bárbara, Colón, Comayagua, and Intibucá.

It soon became apparent that María Esther was trying to do too much. Discussions with Deborah Eade about how María Esther's input could be most effective, as well as about the sustainability of the work, led to a proposal that PAEM produce its own educational materials as a way of making the work with the groups more replicable. The result was *Conociéndome a mi misma*, ('Getting to know myself'), a popular education booklet for use in meetings and the *Guía de la animadora* ('Guide for animators'), a booklet providing guidance in the use of the other booklet and some supplementary materials, such as relevant biblical passages and explanations of issues raised. (Some extracts from these are given at the end of this chapter.) Both booklets arose out of the experience of the women in the groups, and they were involved in determining the content and in the production (for example, in acting for the photographs). The booklets took about three years to produce, and the materials were developed and piloted with the support of Luisa María Rivera, a consultant from Mexico.

Luisa María's work with PAEM was also funded by Oxfam. She had met María Esther when in Honduras doing a consultancy, and they had got on well. Towards the end of the process of developing the booklets, technical support was received from an NGO called COMUNICA which works on media and communication with popular organisations. The booklets were distributed to the various groups, and are still in regular use there as well as being used by other organisations.

Each group consists of up to fifteen women. There was an early decision to keep the groups small, and have more than one group in a community rather than a single large one. This means that each woman can contribute. The groups generally meet weekly, setting their own programmes; meetings start with a recitation of the 'women's prayer' (see opposite).

Sometimes they study a section of *Conociéndome a mi misma*, discussing and reflecting on some aspect of their lives as poor rural women. Each group works independently: some of them take on small projects such as growing vegetables or making *tamales* for sale. They raise small amounts of money to cover any costs the group may incur. Each group chooses two women to act as animators[5] of the group. These women meet with other animators to prepare the themes that will be worked on in the groups and to discuss any issues that arise.

The structure had not been like that from the beginning. The early groups formed after the mission were conventional, with president and

Prayer

God, our mother and father, give refuge to women, particularly to poor women, hard hit today by this way of life which leads us to annihilation and death. Full of hope and faith in Jesus Christ resurrected, we wish to defend our right to life, to dignity, to freedom and to other rights that are ours as people. We want to be bearers of happiness, builders of love, fraternity, justice and peace. We declare our will to unite and co-ordinate our endeavours and to help and support each other. We give thanks to the Holy Spirit for giving us the wisdom, strength and the will which we need in order to build the Kingdom here and now. Amen.

vice-president, secretary, treasurer, and so on. But in 1987 a workshop was held to analyse the organisational structure of PAEM, and it was decided that the traditional form was too vertical, putting too much responsibility onto a few people. It impeded the development of confidence and self-esteem among the rest of the women. An alternative structure was tried briefly, with a team of women filling each of the leadership functions, but that was soon dropped in favour of a more radical change. The notion of having promoters who come in to animate a group from outside was abandoned, and the task is now filled from within the group, and is no longer a permanent task of one person. The groups get together in zonal meetings (there are four zones in Macuelizo) with six to ten other groups; there is a theme and each group brings an activity to share:

...sociodramas [acting out events or situations], *songs, dinámicas* [group exercises], *jokes. Women meet there together and share a moment of entertainment, of good fellowship; we make food to share, we all eat the same food. We learn to be better, to live united, to share our problems and at the same time see what solutions we can find. We do that in the group meetings too.*[6]

A *consejo* (central council) of about 20 women also meets regularly to discuss any issues that arise, analyse and plan activities, and generally play a co-ordinating role. Decisions in this group are taken by a process of consensus, with the decision evolving gradually out of discussion and exploration rather than being voted on.

A series of workshops has enabled PAEM to look at some themes with benefit of support from outside. In the mid-1980s, awareness of gender issues within Honduran NGOs was more or less non-existent. PAEM was helped by a Mexican NGO, *Grupo de Educación Popular para Mujeres* (GEM; Popular Education Group for Women). María Esther had been invited to Mexico by Deborah Eade in 1988, using a special fund set up by Oxfam for exchange visits throughout the region. She met with a number of organisations, including GEM, working in the field of popular education and of women and development in order to find out how they tackled the issues she and PAEM were facing. When the women in PAEM started asking to cover subject areas where she did not have the expertise, she and GEM put together a proposal for the workshop series, to be run by people with experience of working with rural Christian women, and again approached Oxfam for funding. As a result, GEM sent facilitators to run a series of week-long workshops, one a year from 1988 to 1990, on themes such as the role of co-ordinators (as opposed to promoters), gender, gender and sexuality, gender and democracy; they also worked with PAEM on the analysis of their experience. The workshops also helped to address a problem which the women in the groups had begun to identify: María Ester was travelling and making contacts, and her experience should be more widely shared. The workshops were a way of bringing the outside world into the programme.

The evolution of PAEM was not all straightforward. Difficulties arose with the change from an outside promoter to an animator from within the group. There were important differences of opinion between some of the stronger leaders. María Esther was in favour of the more horizontal approach; leaders from the groups in the other departments were less enthusiastic. As a result, some of the groups became more independent and the programme less unified. María Esther focused her PAEM work in Macuelizo. This has opened up new possibilities and there has been a recent attempt to build a network of rural women's organisations across the country, including those previously part of PAEM.

The other main area of difficulty has been in the relations between PAEM and the Catholic Church. The PAEM women identify themselves as Catholic women and the organisation was centred around the church from the beginning. Padre Jesús María, who organised the mission in 1981, was very supportive. As he freely admits, he did not understand what María Esther was trying to do:

I realised that the CARITAS groups weren't making any noticeable advance; they were organising women around certain needs of the parish, but not helping them to excel as women. So I began to see that the work of María Esther was bearing fruit. I began to understand the necessity of a special work with women. But at first I wasn't clear about it... What I did was support them morally. I left the weight of the work in the hands of María Esther and the other women. If they called for a Mass, I went. If there was a problem or difficulty with one of the groups in the community, I would give my support when I went to visit. But I didn't do more than that… I knew the people leading the programme knew where they were going and what methodology to use. I wasn't clear what it was but I knew they were clear. So I supported them. And slowly I saw the results and saw that the method of work was correct. (Padre Jesús María)

The change from promoter to animator also brought María Esther into conflict with women in the parish, one of whom had been a promoter before the change and was also a CARITAS promoter, who saw the work of PAEM as a threat to the functioning of the church and perhaps to her own leadership within it.

In 1991 Padre Jesús María was moved to a different parish in Santa Bárbara, and the incoming priest, Padre Ricardo Pradilla (also a Spanish Passionist) did not share his supportive attitude to PAEM. Padre Jesús María had seen the autonomy of PAEM as a strength, as something that fed the life of the church in Macuelizo, and he had therefore shielded PAEM from a conflict that was beginning to smoulder over their relation to the parish council and other church activities. Padre Ricardo seemed to see PAEM as a threat. It became clear that women would have to choose between their participation in PAEM and their involvement in the church. It was rumoured that the *padre* would not baptise the babies of women who continued in PAEM. According to Padre Ricardo, PAEM was asked to clarify whether they were part of the church or an independent organisation.

For many women, their faith and membership of the Catholic Church are a core component of their identities; it is the thing that helps them to keep going when life feels impossible. As a result of the conflict the number of groups in PAEM in Macuelizo halved, from 30 to 15 in 1991.

This was a difficult time for PAEM; the women were full of doubts and uncertainties; María Esther was under immense pressure. But the women on the *consejo* maintained their unity and have been strengthened by the experience. During the worst of the conflict, in 1992, they went from meeting monthly to meeting once a week, and used the time to voice doubts and express strong emotion as well as to plan and strategise. María Esther had to move into a less visible role because she was the focus for much of the conflict; this meant other women moving forward and taking a firm stand. The personal relationships between the *consejo* members are very strong as a result.

Having survived the conflict, PAEM is facing changes. With the creation of a network of rural Christian women's organisations, Enlace de Mujeres Rurales Cristianas, the programme in Macuelizo needed a more individual identity. This has coincided with a shift in focus of the organisation's work. The educational work will continue, but the women have decided that they are ready now to move on to tackling some of the needs that have been identified. They adopted a new name: Grupo de Mujeres Nueva Esperanza (New Hope Women's Group). The shift in focus is related to the serious problems experienced in the area in the supply of basic grains. PAEM hoped to take over a disused grain warehouse in one of the communities on the paved road, which is part of a national network of warehouses owned by IHMA, the Institute of Agricultural Marketing, funded with European Community economic aid. PAEM negotiated with and received the support of IHMA in the capital, and has located a source of initial funding. As I left in the autumn of 1993, they were tackling the complex local political issues that their plan has raised and applying for legal status as an organisation.

El Pital and Quitasueño

I chose to work in more detail with two strongly contrasting communities, El Pital and Quitasueño, and with the *consejo*.

El Pital is about five miles from the paved road up a steep and winding dirt road in the west of the parish of Macuelizo. It has a population of about 1,100 in about 120 households and is a beautiful village with enough trees left to hide many of the predominantly adobe or *bajareque* houses with thatch roofs that sprawl up the sides of the valley. Some of the houses have concrete floors; some have running water and latrines, but electricity has not yet reached the village. Land is owned by two *campesino* groups (with about 50 members between them and approximately 350 hectares) and by *parceleros*, small landowners of up to 20 hectares. Perhaps a third of the households are landless. The community is well-established — many people were born there — and very well-organised, with most villagers, men and women, being involved in some sort of organisation — the *patronato*, the two *grupos campesinos*, 'base communities' of the Catholic Church, a CNTC women's group, and so on. PAEM has five groups in the community, one of which is a recently formed group for young women. The groups meet separately and have their own activities; they also meet together to study *Conociéndome a mi misma*. Four women from El Pital are on the *consejo*. One of the animators from the groups is a member of and secretary to the *patronato*, and is very active in decision making at the village level.

In El Pital the PAEM groups are lively, and proud of what they do. Most of the women talked easily with me; giving full and thoughtful responses to my questions. Group activities vary: there have been several attempts at collective vegetable plots and *milpas*, most of which have not been very successful. *Superación* runs the motorised mill for the community; *Nuevos Caminos* now has a building, where they cook and sell food.

Quitasueño is a very different community, and one with historical significance for the *campesino* movement. It is situated where the road to El Pital leaves the main paved road. Prior to the formation of the CNTC in 1985, the national *campesino* movement was riven by factionalism. There were five left-of-centre and far-left organisations. The land 'reclamation'[7] that established the *grupos campesinos* in Quitasueño (where previously there had only been a small settlement) was organised by *campesinos* at the grassroots, working across those five organisations, and not by the national leadership. The effect of the land reclamation in Quitasueño was cataclysmic for the national *campesino* movement; the five organisations met and decided to dissolve and to form the CNTC.

A large number of the men of Quitasueño are members of the ten *campesino* groups (co-operatives) that were formed on the 'reclaimed' land. The fact that there are so many *campesino* groups on so little land is a product of the internal politics of the CNTC; although the previous five organisations dissolved, many people still kept their separatist agendas. This community has a history of organising, but without having produced a 'well-organised' community. Various NGOs and church organisations (such as the Mennonites) have also had a presence in the community over the years; this has not resulted in much improvement in people's lives, despite the fact that Quitasueño has good access to markets, being near the main road. Co-op members mostly have well-built cement-block houses, with cement floors, since co-ops have access to official sources of credit. People who are not member of the co-ops live in small adobe or *bajareque* houses with dirt floors. The village has mains electricity and piped water, though not all houses are connected. However, despite apparent material advantages, the position of women in Quitasueño is not noticeably different from that of women elsewhere in the parish. There is one PAEM group, *Fé y Esperanza* (Faith and Hope). There are also CNTC women's groups which operate small shops and undertake other small-scale economic activities.

The PAEM group in Quitasueño was a marked contrast to those in El Pital. The women were very quiet; very few of them participated in the discussion. It seemed clear that the changes achieved in El Pital were not replicated in Quitasueño, despite the use of the same methodology. The PAEM group has undertaken some economic activities as a group, including selling *tamales*, and some of the group run a small shop (not using the identity of the group, and using CNTC funding). Women have not yet moved into public life in the community. Whereas in El Pital, everyone I asked was willing to give their time to talk to me, in Quitasueño my task was much harder. The animators and some members of the group were co-operative; some of the husbands were also happy to talk to me. Others were not. I had several abortive attempts to meet with the *patronato*; there were instances of people failing to keep to agreed arrangements to meet. I had sense that I was seen as an unwelcome and possibly even dangerous intrusion. The differences between the two communities made me realise the significance of the context for processes of empowerment.

What has PAEM achieved?

Although the word 'empowerment' is not used by PAEM (and, in fact, does not exist in Spanish), it is clear that, using the generative view of power as defined in Chapter 2, empowerment is an implicit intention of the programme.[8] While the approach of CARITAS and of other organisa-tions are based on a dependent relationship and on activities that perpet-uate the subordinate position of women, PAEM has attempted to find a different organisational form, and to devise a method of working that will strengthen women's sense of self, and their identities as social and political actors, and help them to identify and meet their own needs The impact of the programme has not been uniform across the groups, but in general has been impressive.

Personal empowerment in PAEM

Almost everyone identified, without prompting, increased levels of confidence and self-esteem in the women as important achievements of the programme. Padre Jesús María described to me the situation before the programme:

Before PAEM the position of women was as it still is for most, as PAEM has changed the lives of some women but not of many. These people are very dependent on someone leading them from in front. Women need someone to tell them what they should be doing. Women have a great capacity for suffering, and a great responsibility for fulfilling their role as mothers. But without the liberty to defend their own rights. I think in the church women feel better; there they are more respected and taken into account. But they are still dependent on the priest and community leaders. If the padre says something you don't question it. Similarly with the delegados [Delegates of the Word]. Many women are still like that as the programme hasn't reached them. (Padre Jesús María)

The changes achieved by the women are very noticeable. Jenny Vaughan, then co-ordinator for CIIR, who first introduced María Esther Ruiz to Oxfam, told me 'When I first went [to visit the communities] it would have been hard to sustain a discussion.' Many women described the changes, often attributing them to 'being organised':

When you're organised you realise things that you didn't know. For example, about women's rights, development; the support there is from other countries. You find out how women aren't considered for anything, you feel you're hardly worth anything. And with the things you study you see that there's support; you gain more strength. You want to meet with the others. The meetings are good. Better to be in a group organised than alone, because no-one explains anything to you. I felt shy; if someone asked me a question I wouldn't know what to say. But in the group that's been leaving me. (Alicia, 31, El Pital)

I felt more confident; happier. If I didn't come to the group I'd be in the house, I wouldn't know anything. It gives me encouragement; you study, you learn. (Elsa, 22, El Pital)

..through becoming organised I have gained knowledge and I have felt an advantage for myself, that I have woken up my mind; because I was a woman who would never speak to a rich person because I was afraid. And today ... whether they have money or not, I speak to people. So you can see that I have left my timidity behind because of being organised. (Esperanza, 47, Quitasueño)

Having the confidence to get out of the house and begin to interact with the world outside is an essential prerequisite to other activities. Most errands outside the home are done by children; once they have children women rarely leave their home unaccompanied by a man. But the notion of 'leaving the house' may also refer to the difference between the private and the public sphere: that through PAEM women have claimed their right to have input and influence outside the immediate limitations of the family.

Before, women never had time, everyone was busy in her home, doing the housework, nothing else, and 'looking out through the cracks' to see who was going by. Now you can see that women have a day to meet each other; on that day she frees herself up, even though she may have other things to do; she knows she must go to the meeting. Before, that space for women didn't exist. (El Pital group)

I've noticed another achievement, that perhaps before there were problems, it made me anxious perhaps to leave here and go to a meeting and now it doesn't make me anxious any more, I go to the meeting and I come back with less timidity. (Quitasueño group)

The isolation of women in the home, where for long periods of time they are alone except for their children, is clearly an obstacle to empowerment processes, and the women of PAEM are well aware of that. When asked what they had done that they wouldn't have done without the groups, the response was:

Perhaps we would have stayed at home [laughter].. *I think that if we'd been only at home, we wouldn't have been able to get more women trained. Because now we're getting trained, through our studies, and we wouldn't have achieved that alone in our homes... 'looking out through the cracks', as the song says.*
(El Pital group)

Women talk about how they started by being quiet and rarely expressing opinions, but over time developed their confidence. The animators encourage each woman to speak, and many group activities are structured to create un-threatening opportunities, using smaller groups for discussion and tasks when the main group is large.

I have seen that there have been a lot of changes, especially when the women here meet, we all participate. Perhaps at first we didn't but now you can see that we all participate. That's an achievement. (Quitasueño group)

As a women who is organised you feel ... stronger, with more courage to be able to speak, because before, when you had never been organised, you don't know what organisation is, you are scared to speak. How were you going to speak to someone you respect? You can't. But now ... I've seen the change that I've made. Before I was very timid and now I'm not; I was too shy to talk with the other women, but now I feel different, I have changed. (Sonia, 34, El Pital)

Women also talked about the importance to them of being able to talk about personal problems, and in particular, to think with the other women about solutions for those problems. In the group they get access to information. The isolation of each woman in her house can be changed; she begins to realise that her individual problems are shared with others. A problem ceases to be an individual shortcoming, and can begin to be seen as a social or political issue that might have causes and solutions outside the four walls of the home. There may also be practical support given, for example if someone falls ill.

A woman on her own, without anyone to help her understand the situation she is living in, she couldn't do anything. ... If we met here, just feeling the things we feel inside without expressing it outside... but no, through the training you start to talk about what you feel, about what you see, with the other women. I haven't forgotten when she [María Esther] told us in a meeting that she had some friends... 'I have some friends who can help me to study' ... that was to encourage us to get organised, so that we would realise that getting together and talking together about problems would help us. (El Pital group)

The increase in confidence and self-esteem is not just something that the women feel and experience for themselves. Changes can also be seen from the outside, as this male community leader describes:

[I] have come to see that they have shown more courage to speak; that they have recognised the rights they have through the training, through the programme of education they've been given. (El Pital *patronato*)

Personal empowerment involves more than increases in confidence and self-esteem; women also need to find ways of having some time for themselves, where all their energy and effort is not going into daily survival and maintenance of the family. The PAEM meetings seem to provide that. It is interesting to find it described as 'rest'.

women never used to have any rest, because they never used to get out of the house for these moments, but now in these moments women have these hours of rest. (El Pital group)

Another aspect of personal empowerment is the development of a capacity to think and analyse, and develop one's own opinions. As confidence gradually increases and women begin to get a sense of their own worth as human beings and as members of the community, their ability to express themselves increases, and so, too, does their ability to understand and when necessary disagree with other people's opinions.

Empowerment in relationships

Padre Jesús María described the normal state of affairs between a couple as follows:

The relation of a woman with her husband is usually complete submission. She fulfils her obligations of faithfulness, always looking after her husband, even when he doesn't reciprocate and doesn't treat her well. But she has obligations to him. So it's an unequal relationship. The man doesn't respect a woman's rights. Not even the woman believes she is entitled to certain rights and to defend them. So often, perhaps for fear of losing the man, or for cultural reasons, from very early it seems they are taught that they have to obey the man; they were married so that she would serve the man... I've always asked myself if in such a relationship there can be affection. I doubt much whether there can be love. There may be to begin with, but it dies, and the woman stays because of her responsibilities as a woman; she's been educated to serve the man. (Padre Jesús María)

For women to empower themselves within such relationships it is clearly necessary to have a sense of personal empowerment; but women also have to develop an understanding that the situation described above is not what they want. For changes to happen in the power dynamics of a close relationship, not only must the woman herself change, but also the other person. Some women have not yet achieved the changes they want:

I can hardly ever go out to the courses I'm supposed to go to because I'm always met with difficulties: 'you have to care for the children', 'how can you leave them with other people who perhaps can't care for them in the same way'; yes, I have problems in all this. (El Pital group)

Some PAEM women spoke of having a bit more liberty:

...we were marginalised by our husbands and now because of the training we've received... you go home and you tell them all about it, so they give [you] a bit more freedom. Not complete freedom, but on the other hand we're not like the marginalised women we were before, they've given us a bit of freedom and that's an achievement... because it was difficult to get it. (Quitasueño group)

They also talked about changes in terms of being able to leave the house — either by getting permission where before it was absent, '*ahora no me impide*' (now he doesn't stop me) or by going out in the absence of permission:

You can see that some of the women are capable of expressing their opinions, even in front of their husbands, of men; opinions that they didn't give before. And to take attitudes they certainly wouldn't have taken before, for example, 'I am going to the meeting even if my husband does get cross'. You would never have seen this attitude before. And you don't normally see this in the CARITAS groups. (Padre Jesús María)

One woman talked about a change in the mood of the relationship — not a dramatic change, but a noticeable difference:

He seems to be a bit milder now, it seems we have more trust in each other, that we talk to each other more, that's what I've achieved. It may be because of old age, but yes, I've seen that he has changed. (Ana María, 42, El Pital)

Such changes often follow long periods of difficulty, as in her case:

... I was an animator for a while when I started, and my husband started on 'damn it, why do they call you so often' and 'damn it, you've been neglecting the house, I didn't get married to have my wife going here and there, I don't like it'. Well, I would say something to him, and in the end I stayed silent. We're not raised to defend ourselves. Perhaps when I had to go out again, I would say 'look, I have to go out on such and such a day to such and such a place because the group has told me we're invited, I'm going to go and I will get someone to stay here, to give you and the kids something to eat and I'm going to go.' Well, sometimes he would say nothing, and sometimes he would put obstacles in my way or get annoyed. In the end it all got too much and he gave me problems with my nerves, 'but you are so ill, you'll get worse if you go, you're no use for this' and later he said to me 'I'm the one who's been messed around, that I have to be battling, spending our money so that you can get better to go and attend

*your study workshops...' he said, 'that is ending up messing you up and it's
messing me up too'. In the end, about two years ago I got depressed, and I had
to completely leave the work co-ordinating the group. I'm still in the group, but
partly to recuperate my health and partly not to be always having problems
with him, perhaps that's why I haven't been able to free myself from that... 'I'll
do this, I'll do that without consent' — I haven't managed that, and I recognise
that it's a serious mistake that he is taking that right from me, that freedom,
but I haven't yet been able to do anything about that.* (Ibid.)

Empowerment in these relationships is a hard struggle for many
women. The tiniest differences become significant when the process of
change is so hard. This woman, who has lived with repeated desertion
and abuse from her husband, was still able to identify something that
was different now from before:

*My husband has been very annoyed and he stayed at home angry if I went out
to meetings and when I came back he said 'better if you were to go once and for
all'. I never would have said that I would have this capacity to go; I always put
up with him and then ... recently he's said 'back then I shouted at you but you
stayed in the organisation, well, stay in it anyway'. Now he doesn't shout at me
but at first he would threaten to punish me.* (Esperanza, 47, Quitasueño)

Achieving one change such as permission to participate does not
necessarily lead on to others:

*He doesn't stop me going to the group. But he doesn't let me be animadora.
But I'd like to do it — to enjoy oneself ... and learn, but he won't let me.*

Q: *And you haven't thought about doing it even if he says no?*

A: [laughter] *Afterwards there would be problems.* (Elsa, 22, El Pital)

Some women have succeeded in more substantive changes in their
relationships with their partner; discussion and negotiation play a central
role in such changes:

*My husband doesn't discourage me. He knows I'm not alone. Also if the man
is organised, the woman should be too. Sometimes I feel discouraged because
of the children, the work. I have support from him. The relationship is always
changing. He gets to know about my rights, discussion; the way of making
agreements when I have to go out and he stays in the house.* (Alicia, 31, El Pital)

*..how to learn to leave the house ... yes, there were serious problems with that.
When we chose someone [to go on a course] it was the first thing we thought,
the thing that made it all more difficult; to leave, to convince the husband and
look for someone to leave the kids with, the hens and all that. And now
whichever woman it is who goes for a week, the man has to have someone to 'do'
for him unless he sees that he can do things himself, that is, unless the man has*

assumed some of the woman's tasks so that she can have the freedom to do other things elsewhere, I think that various women have been achieving some of that. (El Pital group)

Some of the women say that their struggle to be free (as they put it) within their own relationships and homes is a process that will take time and effort — but they are agreed about what they are trying to achieve.

many of the women have achieved a little freedom from their husbands, but things won't finish with that. ... there are still women who haven't been able to achieve complete freedom, to go here and go there without having problems with their husband. The struggle is so big... the power that the husband has over the woman, it's like that all over Latin America and who knows, maybe in much of the rest of the world, and it may always be a bit like that, but that's what we've got a lot of in our people. They oppose it because they say that they have a wife so that she will look after them, when they get home from work, and when the woman wants to go out they don't want to suffer. They don't want even a little bit of it. So it's not over. But you don't have to think we'll always have this struggle for women's liberation, but we can only achieve it through our organisation, through our studies. (El Pital group)

...to go and be away from home for a few days, that's what they don't like, they miss the warmth. [laughter] We have to carry out the struggle in the home, it's getting chilly! (El Pital group)

Some of the men, too, describe changes:

... now let's say, a woman has authorisation to go where she wants, all over. It's good that the man doesn't forbid her the activities she has a right to. Before he didn't let her go out of the house, so something has been achieved. (El Pital *patronato*)

There's more dialogue about what they must do. It's different now. There are changes in them. You can discuss things. We talk about things now; before we didn't agree; now we discuss. I don't oppose her going out. (Enrique, husband of Miriam, 42)

The men see that there is some dialogue that didn't exist before:

A:*...perhaps in some, or perhaps in all homes, if you're going to do some work you communicate first with your wife about what you are going to do and when you're going to do it. You plan the time and develop the work as well.*

Q: *And if she isn't in agreement with something that happens?*

A: *You'd have to look for a way of seeing if you'll do something else or if you'll not do it at all. You make an agreement, because if the lady isn't agreed that you do the work, if she doesn't give her support, you can't do the work.*

Q: *And how would it have been before?*

A: *Well... it's said that the man used a lot of machismo, right; the man said he was going to do a thing even though to her it didn't seem [right]... but she said nothing, she had to do what the man told her to do. So it was just the man's decision.* (El Pital *patronato*)

They know how to live with the family, there's more dialogue with the family, about how people should behave, the rights they have. Before this had been denied. Perhaps it offends you that the woman is in a group. At the beginning one doesn't even want to be in a group oneself. We think they'll say things against men. But no. It's a training. At least we talk about the ways to resolve things. Before I would have done the administration of the home; now we collaborate, both. Also you can see the development of the family. Health. Improvement in hygiene. Many things they've done. You don't see this when there aren't groups. Women are oppressed, not appreciated. Men and women have the same rights. They must both think about the problems for the household. It's hard in practice.. there's no tradition, so it costs to change.
(Javier, husband of Guadalupe, 44)

Most of the men were themselves members of *grupos campesinos* and there is some evidence that men are more open to change in the relationship if they themselves are 'organised'. The men in the *grupos campesinos* seem to be able to perceive the benefits of women also organising — although these may be seen in terms of the woman 'being a better wife and mother' as a result. However, women whose husbands were not in groups also reported being able to go out more freely, so the evidence is by no means conclusive.

The possibility of negotiation changes the nature of the relationship. When 'power-over' was used by the man in decision making, the woman's response to his actions would be submission or resistance. Once it is established that responsibility is shared, the woman has a new kind of power in the situation and shares the responsibility that goes with that:

...perhaps there wasn't any place for dialogue. So they couldn't discuss things, if he was going out, or if there was going to be some disaster over something he planned to do. But instead ... for example if some work hasn't turned out right, the woman can't accuse the man over it because it was a decision of both of them to do the work, and the man can't blame the woman because the two of them decided together. If things turn out well, so much the better. (El Pital *patronato*)

Empowerment can also be experienced in other close relationships, with children, parents, and in-laws:

...there's a change at home because now if I tell my children I'm going to go somewhere now they know where they will be, now they are aware and don't

put obstacles in my way ... And also my husband does a few things so that I can go. So I've achieved that change in the home. (El Pital group)

Collective empowerment: the PAEM groups

The PAEM groups have acted as the vehicle for much of the process of personal empowerment; they have also enabled the women to create an identity, and provided a basis from which to act in the world. Padre Jesús María again:

I realised that women were growing; that they weren't just meeting in order to have some project but they were growing as people, they had more ability to decide for themselves. For example, they organised the assemblies, their team, their management; before, the priest or a nun would have done it. And I began to see the maturity in the thinking of certain women, at least of those who were leading the groups, and later in the women in the groups. I saw that they had an identity different from the other women in the community.

These women were capable of taking decisions that other women wouldn't have taken. I suppose that they were developing an awareness based on what they did when they met, themes about their situation, their oppression as women, machista culture, and how to help their husbands... they were becoming aware that the way they had been living hadn't helped them or anybody. They had meetings, marches, assemblies, did plays; and all this was about women's issues. I think this raised their consciousness; all these meetings and so on gave them an identity. (Padre Jesús María)

Each PAEM group decided for itself what kind of activities it would undertake in addition to the study programme: small income or food-generating activities such as growing corn and beans, making and selling *tamales*, and so on. Each group took charge of raising the income needed to enable it to participate in the wider PAEM activities, and some also raised money for themselves:

... we did beans, and with the sacks of beans we sold we bought more sacks of beans which we stored and in the season when they sell at a good price we sold them. So we managed to buy some land at 150 lempiras for a manzana and we cultivated coffee. Then a part of it was ruined, a pest got into another part of it, and we harvested the remaining quarter of it that was good and from that we shared out the proceeds a bit for each one of us. (Teresa, 50, El Pital)

Not all income-generating activities were successful. But they ensured that each group took responsibility for itself, and also enabled the groups to construct an identity visible to the wider community.

... we knew what was happening to us and that we had to find our own solutions. People from outside couldn't do that for us.. perhaps they would only

know what we had told them about things, but the people who knew about our problems were us. (Teresa, 50, El Pital)

Friendships have developed which have nourished the group as well as the individuals. The process of developing the text of *Conociéndome a mi misma* and the *Guía de la Animadora* and their subsequent use contributed both to group identity and self-respect.

In terms of collective empowerment, the crucial achievement of the PAEM groups has been the development of a sense of collective agency and purpose; of an identity and understanding of themselves as groups of people who could act in the wider community, taking charge on their own terms of what they did. Padre Jesús María described this:

For example, this problem of needing marketing of basic grains. So they think about it and decide whether to do it or not to do it. The problem they have now with the priest: other groups wouldn't have faced up to the problem; a CARITAS group that has problems stops meeting and ends; but these groups have main-tained themselves, and are achieving a strong maturity. In the face of problems, they look for solutions, they don't ask others for the solutions or abandon the group because of the problem. ...they've taken the decisions. They see what's necessary and look for how to achieve it. They're walking on their own two feet. (Padre Jesús María)

In order to achieve this sense of agency, the women had to decide to ignore any gossip about them. They were, for example, often referred to by their detractors as being involved in *hechería* (witchcraft). In El Pital, where a majority of women in the community are in PAEM groups, their purpose actively included the development of new groups:

We organised the group that Janda is in; from there we set about organising the 'Women on the March' group; After organising that, well, there were more women who weren't organised. We went to communicate with them then we went out to find more women, enrolling them until we organised the other group. Well, now we had four groups. But the young women were not organised. In the assembly they suggested that there should be a group just of young women, so we called the young women together and we enrolled them too.
(Teresa, 50, El Pital)

Collective empowerment: the PAEM consejo

The women who have made up the PAEM *consejo* have gone through an additional process of empowerment. As well as being animators of their groups, they have met regularly in a group with a different purpose, that of providing leadership and co-ordination. Because of the different nature of the *consejo* group, the outcomes have a different quality: the effects are greater, the levels of self-confidence higher, the sense of agency and purpose more pronounced.

Meetings of the PAEM *consejo* were held in María Esther's house. Fifteen to eighteen women and a variable number of young children would arrive any time from 8.00am onwards; by 10.00am everyone would have arrived, having come on foot or by bus from the various communities. If the weather was fine the meeting would be held outside under a spreading tamarind tree. If not, the women would stay inside, squeezed into the largest room in the house. The meetings were very efficiently run, with one woman facilitating (this job rotated). First would be the recitation of 'the women's prayer'. Then, after the minutes of the last meeting had been read, an agenda would be put together and then steadily worked through, with a break for lunch. The meetings had an atmosphere of goodwill and friendship, with many jokes and much laughter. Everyone participated actively. All opinions were respectfully listened to and considered.

Before I attended a meeting of the *consejo*, I had heard criticisms of Maria Esther's dominance of the PAEM programme. It was interesting, therefore, to find that at the first meeting I attended, Maria Esther spent most of her time preparing the lunch. The meeting proceeded without her, the group making decisions when necessary and planning for the future. At subsequent meetings I attended, her participation was greater; but there were always times when she was quiet, or absent, and her absence did not seem to impede the proceedings.

The women in the *consejo* have developed not only confidence but impressive abilities to analyse and plan. Some were already active outside the home before the programme started; others were not. As animators they receive some training in the form of regular preparation sessions for the study of *Conociéndome a mi misma*; as *consejo* members there is no formal training and they learn as they go along.

When there were tasks to be done, a small group, or perhaps an individual, would be delegated to do them and report back to the next meeting. There was no immediately discernible difference between their willingness to take on mundane tasks or tasks that involved travelling to negotiate with a government official in Santa Bárbara — except where child-care was a relevant factor. Discussions in the *consejo* showed a good knowledge of and interest in local and national politics. When there were obstacles to be overcome, there was a sense that something would always be possible. While I was there the negotiations about the grain warehouse were under way. They originally hoped to take over the one in Sula, not far from Casa Quemada, on the main road. Local politics defeated that, as Sula, in its attempt to become a *municipio* in its own right, needed somewhere to put the prerequisite secondary school, and took over the building. Undeterred, the *consejo* worked out an alternative plan, to take over the more derelict building in Quitasueño. This involved them in a much more complex situation, facing active opposition from some of the *campesino* groups and the CNTC.

The process of collective empowerment of the *consejo* has included learning to obtain and manage resources. María Esther was responsible for the original application for funding to Oxfam and then the Catholic Fund for Overseas Development (CAFOD). In order to obtain general funding for a further three years from Oxfam, and a significant sum from CAFOD for the grain warehouse project, other members of the *consejo* had put together the application and budget (on which they were congratulated). The application was submitted later than they had intended, but María Esther did not give in to the temptation to step in and help them with it. She told me she felt it was better that they learn for themselves, and they would just have to manage for a while without the money. The treasurer is a *consejo* member who is very meticulous, and who has learned to manage the money 'on the job', with support from María Esther.

The *consejo* meetings provide a forum for leadership development. After each series of zone meetings detailed reports are given. If the animators co-ordinating one of the zone meetings were not happy with some aspect of the meeting, they describe the problem to the *consejo*, and then there is a discussion. For example, there had been insufficient food at one of the zone meetings, and claims that it had not been handed out fairly. It was a hot issue, and the discussion went on for about half an hour. They worked out that the problem had several causes: some people would come back for a second portion before others were served; a number of women would come to eat who weren't actually at the meeting and hadn't been catered for; it was also difficult to estimate the right size for portions. They decided that they needed to reflect on the problem with all the women in the groups and work towards people having a position of respect so that each of these problems would stop. 'Collective reflection' on the problem, with everyone involved in thinking about the difficulties and possibilities, was seen as important. By tackling the issue in this way, both in the *consejo* meeting and in the groups, the animators were able to think the problem through for themselves and work out a strategy to tackle it, and then to tackle it with their own group — knowing they had the support of the other *consejo* members.

Collective empowerment: outside PAEM

In several of the communities where PAEM has been active, the women's groups have been entering into active relationships with other community organisations. In El Pital, one of the women is now in the *patronato*. The women's groups there have become very visible in the community in a way they were not before PAEM started. According to the *patronato*, Padre Jesús María and María Esther, changes have been considerable. There used to be no women in the *directivas* of any of the community organisations. Now as well as the aforementioned woman secretary to the *patronato*, there are four women officers in the *Sociedad de Padres de Familia* (Parents Society). The membership of the latter is now half female whereas before it was all male. Each of the *grupos campesinos* now has one woman full member. It was the men I interviewed, and the members of the *patronato*, who were clearest about the significance of this change. Women who were always quiet, if they ever went to public meetings, now participate and express opinions. The PAEM women have also succeeded in enlisting the support of other community organisations when they need it. One of the groups had a conflict with a local teacher. The women had built a small building to use for cooking and selling food; the teacher's land adjoined theirs, and when they built a fence, he knocked it down again repeatedly. They took the case to the municipal authorities in Macuelizo, who ruled in the teacher's favour. So the women went to the *patronato* and the *campesino* groups for support, with the result that the teacher left the community.

In another community, Trascerros, the PAEM group was involved in a dispute with the municipality of Macuelizo, which wants to resolve a serious water supply problem for the town of Macuelizo by piping water from one of the rivers at Trascerros, some ten miles away. The people of Trascerros were apparently not consulted over this, and were very concerned that their own water supply would be insufficient as a result of the proposed scheme. The women of Trascerros have led the opposition to the scheme, and have mobilised the community and pushed for further meetings. It seemed unlikely that the women would succeed in their campaign; but what is important in terms of the empowerment process is that they now perceive themselves as able to act, and to be a force to be reckoned with in the wider community, ready to confront the political authorities in the region.

In connection with the grain warehouse project, PAEM is now able to negotiate with national organisations, such as the Honduran Institute for Agricultural Marketing, IHMA, which is in charge of the grain warehouses. IHMA decided to support the women's application: 'the organisation has maturity; they're not moving forward because they have no productive project. They have capable people, if we give them training. ...Yes, we have confidence in them.' (Raúl Contrera) The women have experience of working with Oxfam and CAFOD, and also with the ODA who supplied some of the funding via Oxfam. However, as María Esther explained to me, they do not intend to limit their contacts with external agencies to the small and familiar:

... we thought, well, we've had training now, so we are going to negotiate a project to initiate work on our survival needs. We have to develop a capacity for negotiation and the project will be negotiated with the government, with the United Nations, and we are not going to ask Oxfam or CAFOD, because ... their role is to contribute to the first step, to help us to lift ourselves out of the crushed state we have been in historically. And this year we are going to start. That is to say we are in the middle of formulating the project and we are opening a space for negotiation with the United Nations. We'll see what happens.
(María Esther)

Relationships with the Catholic Church locally have been problematic since Padre Jesús María left. But PAEM has better relationships with the church further afield. This is largely due to María Esther's personal relationships with various church organisations, priests and bishops. (She was invited to present a paper at the Latin American Bishops conference in Colombia in 1992.) So PAEM, through the person of María Esther, has access to an influential source of power in the wider community.

Another example of collective empowerment reaching outside PAEM and the local community is the *Enlace de Mujeres Cristianas Rurales*. Having moved to make the PAEM groups in other parts of the country separate and autonomous, the women have decided to create an organisation that can function on a national level and can provide a collective voice for rural women. *Enlace* is still a very young organisation, and it is largely the brain-child of María Esther; but she is determined not to be the only leader — in fact, she insisted on not being on its committee — and the Macuelizo women are keen to see the new network take shape.

PAEM, then, has enabled the women participants to move collectively and individually into new areas of activity and influence. In Chapter Six I shall explore what it was that made such changes possible.

An analysis of empowerment in PAEM

The process of empowerment involves change, in the personal dimension, collectively, and in relationships. PAEM has been successful in generating empowerment among the women in the programme. Why and how did this happen? To answer this question, we will consider a number of factors: the role of particular individuals, the external support the programme received, the methodology used, the underlying philosophy, the style of leadership, and the effect of the conflict.

Significant individuals

There is no doubt that PAEM has succeeded because of the personal qualities of María Esther Ruíz. Not only did she provide the initial momentum, but also the approach and the skills that have enabled it to grow and survive. She is herself a *campesina*, and a local woman, having been born in Casa Quemada and lived in the area for most of her life. This is an important factor: the programme was neither dreamt up nor implemented by outsiders. Local women could see that, although she had had opportunities to develop skills and abilities that they had not had, she was one of them and understood their situation. Her thinking and analysis, and therefore her proposals for action, came out of that understanding, and the women could trust her and her judgement about what they needed to do without suspending their own judgement.

Another significant factor is María Esther's skill and experience as a community and political activist. Her years as a worker and leader within the church, the CNTC, and the radio schools have earned her the respect of local, regional, and national leaders of those movements, including those who disagree with her. She was known in the region, and had a wealth of contacts to draw on. She also had good local knowledge, understanding well the dynamics and activities of the various organisations operating in the area.

A third quality María Esther brought to the work with PAEM was a fierce commitment to the work and to the women. She was able and willing to fight hard to resist pressures to hand over the groups to other organisations (many non-government and popular organisations needed to be able to show they were working with women), and to withstand the intense pressure and stress of the conflict with the parish priest, in which she was the target of much attack and gossip.

Padre Jesús María also had significant influence. His initial personal and intellectual support and encouragement to María Esther were important, and he protected the women's groups when they were new:

He gave her the space to work, to develop groups, put theory into practice. They had a strong intellectual relationship. María Esther has had a very rigorous training. Jesús María didn't always understand, but he was prepared to support her work because he could see gender inequities and that CARITAS hadn't worked, and he could see the changes in women's confidence and ability to participate. Jesús María was very important in mediating between María Esther and the CNTC (which was very hostile to the work). (Jenny Vaughan)

He supported the autonomy of PAEM, and he encouraged the formation of the *consejo*:

... in order to form the consejo we also consulted Padre Jesús when he was in Macuelizo and he helped us form it, he told us it was a good idea that we had, because that way we would be able to achieve more within the church and with faith. (El Pital group)

External support

Both PAEM as an organisation and María Esther as an individual have received support from outside the programme that has made the establishment, growth and survival of the programme possible. It is not only the financial support but also the relationship with the funding bodies that has been important. María Esther was not willing to compromise the nature of PAEM, or to adjust the programme to fit a funding agency's agenda, in order to receive funding:

...we haven't been able to establish relations with other agencies because of our own character... we don't fall within the criteria of the agencies or the methodology they use. (María Esther)

In Oxfam they found an agency that was willing to take risks and be flexible; to support a different approach to work with women; to work with a structure that was not the usual 'three-year project'. This allowed PAEM to respond to the needs of the women as they identified them and at their own pace. (As it turned out, that pace was faster than María Esther had anticipated, as she had thought it might take up to ten years to get the women in the communities to the point where they would be initiating their own solutions.) But Oxfam was willing to work slowly.

Support also came in the form of an advisor, Luisa María Rivera, an ex-nun and a social worker. Having someone with whom she could discuss her work and explore ideas was very helpful to María Esther

...she knew her way round the kind of environment that María Esther was working in very well indeed, and that was important. We wouldn't have sent just anybody; and it happened that they hit it off very well and established a level of trust in each other that went beyond expectations. That was something that Oxfam as a funding agency wouldn't have given María Esther; there was no way that I could sit down with one project holder as long as Luisa María did with her; and also I don't have the skills and I didn't have the knowledge; but I did have the contacts so that was what essentially I put at María Esther's disposal. And then out of that the two of them started to work exclusively on producing the booklet, 'Conociéndome a mi misma'... (Deborah Eade)

Personal support was also forthcoming to María Esther from a wide range of contacts; some individual feminists working for development agencies became personal friends and gave much moral support as well as opportunities for the exchange of ideas. PAEM was being set up at a time when NGOs in general were gender-blind in Honduras, and PAEM was being seen as divisive or as falling outside the (rigid) definition of the popular movement and therefore as not relevant. At this time, Honduran feminism had hardly developed.[9] Her outside contacts provided encouragement, and enabled María Esther to develop her analysis beyond the point where most Hondurans were ready to go.

Further support came with the workshops run by the Mexican women's organisation, GEM. The workshops were very effective in helping the women work out new ideas. The presence of outsiders also provided a form of external validation to the women and their work. Technical support was provided by COMUNICA in the production of the booklets and of a short video on PAEM. This happened at the time of the conflict with the priest, and helped the women, and María Esther in particular, to survive that difficult period.

As the programme developed, a number of men in the communities became allies. Deliberate work with men has not been part of the programme, but men have been welcomed at zone meetings and many of them participated in a big rally that took place at the time of the conflict. María Esther has had good support from her husband, himself a well-known community activist.

Philosophy

One of the strengths of the PAEM programme in terms of empowerment is the explicit attitude that poor rural women are capable of taking charge of their lives. The programme's philosophy is egalitarian and feminist. Its feminism comes not out of an intellectual analysis of inequality, but out of María Esther's analysis of women's rights as human beings to take part in change on their own terms. Again, Deborah Eade:

she was saying, and she didn't have the words to say it with, that the personal is political. She was recognising, because that was where she herself had come from, that the way in which women are oppressed gets right into their souls, right into their lack of self-esteem, the fact that they don't think of themselves as having human rights, let alone civil, political, or social rights of any kind, and that was her starting point. (Deborah Eade)

As María Esther sees it, if women participate as protagonists in development on their own terms, a different analysis is reached about what needs to happen:

*she believes so profoundly that it is women themselves who are going to have
to transform gender relations; they can't have them transformed for them; they
themselves are going to have to be the agents of change in their own favour.
And she has an absolute clarity about that, where other people will tend to
say, 'Oh well that's how it is', or 'Oh well that's natural', or 'Oh well that's
cultural', and therefore 'No me toca' [it's not my business to interfere].* (Ibid.)

María Esther believes that if the quality of the work is good, it will
spread outwards of its own accord; she is therefore not too concerned with
quantity. The philosophy has been one of letting things take their own
time; of not forcing the pace of change. There is recognition that empowerment (although that word was not used by PAEM) may be a slow process,
and part of that process is for women to work at their own pace and not be
pushed into taking things on for which they are not ready.

The other main aspect of the philosophy of PAEM is its rootedness in
Catholicism. There is a strong belief that all human beings are created
equal in the eyes of God, and a concomitant fierce belief in human rights,
that is informed by Liberation Theology. There is a belief also that
women are excluded from exercising their human rights if they are
oppressed. The women in the PAEM communities are strongly Catholic
and their faith provides them with an anchor in their lives. The church
has been one of the few places where women are valued and have a role;
it has also provided one of the few reasons for women to be able to leave
the house, and to exist as something other than wives and mothers. The
work of PAEM built on that spiritual validation, transforming it into a
general validation of women, their abilities and their work. The element
of faith and spirituality in the programme gives the women access to a
kind of 'power to' which springs from 'power within', in the form of a
source of energy, renewal, and commitment, particularly in adversity.

So PAEM has been working with a philosophy that both expects
women to be able to think and act, and which puts them in charge of the
process of change. Given the weight of the existing culture that
communicates the opposite message, this philosophy has been crucial in
creating an environment where empowerment can happen.

Methodology

The methodology of the programme encourages and contributes to the
empowerment process. There is an emphasis, in the materials and the
way the groups run, on helping women to create a concept of themselves
as active agents. Deborah Eade comments on this:

*what was innovative was [María Esther's] grasp of the fact that for things to
change, and for this to be a participative process, actually required everybody to*

hold responsibility; but that building up the capacity to hold that responsibility is a very, very long haul indeed. Because you have to start with people having a sense of themselves as human beings... When I was in Honduras in 1992, I saw COMUNICA's video of PAEM's work. I was very moved. Here were women whom I'd met in 1986, and who at that time couldn't speak without covering their mouths with their hands and saying 'soy muy tímida para hablar' ['I am very nervous of speaking'], addressing the camera or a crowd of women. And they had become people who were assertive, and as strong as they'd always potentially been, but now able to live and project this strength; and that was just fantastic. I've not seen anything like it in any other popular education work. (Deborah Eade)

Eventually that concept of self can come to include a sense of being able to take responsibility for what happens and deciding to act. To build this capacity may require a willingness to focus on very personal and apparently trivial issues in women's everyday lives. Take, for example, the worry that a child is falling ill. This is the kind of thing that will preoccupy a woman and make it hard for her to participate in other activities. Within the PAEM methodology, the situation can be analysed in group or zone meetings or in discussion between individual group members. The analysis may raise questions such as: why is the child falling ill? Why does it preoccupy mothers so much? What support can we give each other, such as sharing what we know about treatments, or helping each other to get the medical resources we need? How could we help prevent the illness? Through discussion, women analyse the situation, gather information, express their feelings, and receive support, develop new understandings and perspectives, and act.

Also important, both in terms of the empowerment process and in terms of the survival of the programme, has been the focus on changes that women could feel in their own lives. They were encouraged to work, not towards some change that might happen in the future, but on areas where they could begin to make changes right away, in their relationships with their families, with each other, and with the community. These changes may not have been visible to the outsider — in fact many people outside the groups, including husbands, commented that the groups 'did nothing'. They certainly were not doing the normal kinds of development activity. But the women themselves kept coming to the groups: they would not have done so if they were getting nothing from them.

Another central aspect of the PAEM methodology is its emphasis on the need to combat the isolation that many women feel. This is achieved physically by getting women together, and intellectually by encouraging the sharing of ideas and experiences. As a consequence, women develop confidence and self-esteem; they begin to receive positive feedback, perhaps for almost the first time. They begin to learn to think for themselves, to acquire information, to develop a sense of the wider context within which they live, and to have an aim and purpose outside their immediate families.

The methodology includes the encouragement of total respect for each individual, for each person's right to *dignidad* — which, in Spanish, conveys more than the literal translation, 'dignity', and includes self-respect, self-esteem, and a sense of being not only worthy of respect from others, but having a right to that respect. This is clearly brought out in *Conociéndome a mi misma* and was evident in the various meetings that I attended. For women to take power in aspects of their own lives, especially where this requires a struggle, self-respect is essential, or the individual gives in when faced with opposition. Many women have a low opinion of themselves, and I heard many instances of women in the groups criticising themselves and each other. This can be seen as an internalisation of oppression, of the experience of having been treated badly, of feeling powerless, of having no rights and not deserving to be treated well. Part of the empowerment process is learning to stop criticising others and oneself. Women in the *consejo* rarely spoke disparagingly, and often expressed appreciation of each other.

One of the aspects of methodology on which María Esther insisted from the beginning was that of the women identifying their own needs and ways of satisfying those needs. Identifying needs was not simply a matter of saying what was needed; it involved a process of self-examination and of understanding the circumstances of their lives. This, crucially, included learning about their position as women, and their rights as women. Thus in El Pital:

...in the group, that is where we talk among ourselves about what we have to do, how we are going to do it, and what we want to do, like 'how could we improve our life?' Because what we want is that we should have good health, good housing. We talk about all those things ... about what we have to do to get from here to there, and about what we know. Because sometimes things happen and you don't get to know about them when you're closed in alone, but together things can be solved, even though the things you suffer are unbearable.
(Teresa, 50, El Pital)

It also included learning about 'forbidden' subjects, and in particular, sexuality, which is an area where women are particularly constrained — and not the kind of thing often touched on in a standard development project. In these areas, too, the women identified their own agenda:

what [María Esther] did was to have workshops where people did tell her some pretty difficult home-truths and out of these they would devise an agenda for what work needed to be done. Women themselves had said that sexuality was something they wanted to discuss; though she, probably in a rather prudish sort of way, hadn't thought it was so central, but women themselves were saying 'we're totally dominated by our sexuality, we don't have freedom of choice, we have children whether we want them or not, this is a way in which we are oppressed'. (Deborah Eade)

It was important that the women not only identified their own needs, but that the methodology encouraged and enabled them to probe beyond their immediate and readily-identified needs to see what lay behind those. That required a degree of introspection and discussion of personal issues, and it was important that the skills were available to help them with that work. There was no automatic acceptance of 'what we need is a goat project'; the identified need must be deconstructed first. (Why is it that we think we need goats? Why is that the solution we see? Is there perhaps some other way of meeting the hidden need behind that idea? Who would be in control of such a project? Are other people doing the same? What has been their experience? What problems might there be? And so on.)

Most of the meetings I attended, of the groups and of the *consejo*, were punctuated by laughter. Occasionally there were also tears. The methodology of PAEM encourages the women to talk about and express their feelings. Expressing emotion in this way is one means of undoing the effects of internalised oppression; if people can express the emotion rather than suppressing it, they can think more flexibly and creatively about what they want and need and how to get it.[10]

Creativity as well as discussion is used in the groups: the local groups prepare *sociodramas*, drawings and poems for the zone meetings and assemblies as a way of expressing their ideas. Including creativity, and by inference, enjoyment, as part of the methodology seems to help the process of empowerment. If people enjoy themselves they are more open to developing ideas and to trying out new things. The use of humour as a weapon against the powerful can make them seem less formidable.

PAEM is a women-only programme, which is appropriate for the cultural context. In order to participate anywhere near equally in a mixed programme within a *machista* culture, women have to have already empowered themselves significantly. Otherwise, as can be seen in many of the mixed programmes that exist in Honduras and other Latin American countries, women will be silent and scarcely participate beyond being physically present. In the women's groups they are able to develop the skills and the confidence they need for participating in mixed organisations — which some PAEM women are now doing. Their women-only identity as an organisation does not, however, preclude the inclusion of men in some of their activities, and this has been important in not isolating the organisation from the wider community.

The early work of PAEM was firmly under the wing of the Catholic Church. As the groups developed, PAEM established a form of 'protected autonomy', encouraged by Padre Jesús María, which then became full autonomy.[11] This meant that the women could take the time they needed to develop their leadership and organisational capacity. This has been of crucial importance in allowing them to develop their own way of tackling issues, some of which the church doctrine might not condone.

The PAEM programme has provided to many women the opportunity to move physically out from their own communities into the wider world. The annual assemblies and the zone meetings serve this purpose for the women in the groups. For the women in the *consejo* there are also opportunities to attend conferences in other parts of the country. This moving outwards contributes to the growth of confidence and self-esteem; it also gives access to information and the chance of sharing experience with other women in similar or different positions. In the case of the *consejo* members, it provides the opportunity to learn about a range of new issues and to be active in negotiation and other activities. The experiences are not always positive; for example, PAEM women had a difficult time at the first Central American feminist meeting, as they disagreed with some ideas considered fundamental to feminism by others.

A more controversial aspect of the methodology is the organisation of the programme in a way which did not immediately fill an economic, income-generating purpose. Many people have argued that any development work with poor women must make some contribution to meeting their economic needs if they are to be able to make the time available to participate. Because of this, many women's organisations have focused on donated food. María Esther was strongly against this form of encouraging dependency:

I wanted to test the thesis and see if it was true, that women will only get together if they are given things. And the experience of Macuelizo has shown us otherwise. That we poor women have the capacity to meet with others to think about ourselves, not only over projects; that has been proved. On the other hand, we've also shown that projects must respond to urgent needs and problems, identified by women themselves. For us the first problem was women's lack of organisational confidence, [lack of] education, the way they are devalued by themselves and by society. (María Esther)

Deborah Eade agrees:

... it's a commonplace that very poor people haven't got the time and energy to do social organisation work. They've got to have their basic needs met first and

then they can give themselves the luxury to think about human rights. In my experience it's totally the reverse. That it is precisely when people had nothing — for example, those suffering extreme repression and hardship, such as in El Salvador — that they would insist that ensuring respect for their human rights, their social, civil, and political rights, was the guarantee without which their material needs could not be met in a sustainable way. (Deborah Eade)

So the methodology was designed to avoid the relationships of dependency which are so embedded in Honduran culture. María Esther again:

They didn't go to the group to receive things; they went to talk about themes. It's not easy to find the cause of an effect. Possibly there were many reasons for all this. One I've seen is that women who before were always dependent on the priest, and who didn't do things if no one gave them the money — these women were capable of taking their own decisions. Normally women's groups, like those in other parishes that I've seen or heard of, if the promoter isn't there, they don't meet. There aren't actions if there's no-one telling them what needs to be done. The working of the programme — it's not the responsibility of the women — sometimes they don't even know about their programme, or where it is going. (María Esther)

It was not that María Esther did not believe in the need for income-generating projects. But her experience with CARITAS and other organisations had left her sceptical of what such small projects can achieve:

Small projects won't resolve our problems; we need big projects. A few seeds or a shop with 1,000 pesos invested isn't going to make a difference. That allows us to say we have something, but doesn't resolve anything. There is no grain marketing in the region; no organisation is interested in basic grains; it's a real problem. That would stabilise prices. At least in our groups there would be grain at a fair price. ...With the shops people stay isolated; there's no regional organisation. And it maintains vertical relationships. The isolated group with a small shop in a community ... they don't build relationships between women. It is the promoter who makes relationships with everyone; and it's the leaders who relate to everything... and I ask myself, why don't they let us talk, why don't they let us know each other? Because this gives another dimension, and this gives power... and those people interested in power are not going to permit it. (María Esther)

So by María Esther's decision, the programme set out to work with women in a way which would move them towards having the capacity and confidence to tackle a larger project — which they are now doing. In terms of the empowerment process, this illustrates the importance of having a larger vision of what might be achieved.

The fact that the programme was not linked to income generation also meant that the women had the opportunity to practise organising, running events, and to take on the tiny economic activities in the different groups in a way that let them make mistakes without putting their economic well-being at risk. They could learn and develop their organising skills. The fact that there was no insistence on specific quantitative performance indicators on the part of the funding agencies also helped, as there was no pressure to meet specific targets.

Leadership style

A structural factor that plays an important role, both in developing the sense of collective agency and in encouraging personal empowerment and the general effectiveness of the groups, is the approach to leadership. At the beginning, María Esther, as the main initiating force of the programme, provided the leadership. She knew, however, that she did not want to perpetuate the model of a single powerful leader:

...I had, so to speak, a responsibility to co-ordinate... what the programme was, as a process of initiating and training leadership. My primary task was to facilitate... to 'accompany' the training of leadership using a new conception of what leadership is. That is, a new style of leadership both at the level of the co-ordinating team as the programme then was, and at the level of the animators in the case of Macuelizo. (María Esther)

She planned to do herself out of a job:

...to remove the necessity for me to be there. If I'm there, the compañeras won't assume responsibility. And I am concerned that they do assume it, they've been trained for that; there is no one who will say now that 'no, they're not ready'. (María Esther)

She believes that the form of leadership is very relevant to the empowerment of women, and did not want the programme to adopt a leadership model that would perpetuate a sense of dependency or powerlessness:

If you start a project with three co-ordinators you don't have conflict with anyone. Women don't meet each other... If they meet each other and organise — and have a big demonstration and so on — these women are going to have power. Now it is clear that NGOs and the church don't strengthen the self-management of women, because then they won't be able to take the decisions. (María Esther)

The shift from having external promoters to having animators from within the groups demonstrated to all the women that they were potentially capable of taking leadership; it also, claims María Esther, pushed the women out of old habits of dependency:

...when we have full-time staff it gets in the way; on the one hand they contribute; but on the other hand they prevent more women from getting involved: 'there are already people doing it, why should I get involved?' So how to create an atmosphere of shared responsibility? There has to be a structure that permits it. (María Esther)

The women in the groups discussed the issues and told me that they were aware of the dangers of the old model:

...we know that people from outside are not going to come and solve our problems. So it's us then — because you could have a promoter, and we'd just be there complaining. We saw that the animators were very important now; each group had its animator, and it was the animators who had to help the group develop, that was when we were really taken into account. (Teresa, 50, El Pital)

The women taking leadership were supported by their group and by the process of training and interaction with other animators.

...they gave us a short course of three days, that's how we trained. And at the end of the month we were giving the training to all the groups. (Ibid.)

After the formation of the *consejo*, that group functioned as a leadership support group as well as a planning and co-ordinating body. This allowed them to take risks and to learn from any mistakes made. It also helped them to avoid the temptation to fall into the old model of 'power over' leadership, which would impede the empowerment process for the other women in the groups.

The challenge for this style of leadership is for the original leader to find a way of stepping back and handing over power to the new leaders. When the initial leader is as charismatic as María Esther this can be a problem, especially in interactions with the outside world, where people have expectations not only that the old model of leadership will continue, but that the particular individual will be the person they relate to. The process of transition for PAEM has not been entirely smooth, but appears to be succeeding. María Esther's own determination and commitment to change is essential for this. It is one reason why the PAEM programme was officially ended, so that a new beginning could be made:

The programme has finished. It has now ended. It finished in 1992... I didn't want to make a funding application last year, because I had no more interest in that, and I realised that I didn't want to carry on in a co-ordinating role; I'd rather wait for the group to get on with making its own decisions, taking its own responsibility. (María Esther)

María Esther has provided the initiating leadership in the new national network of rural Christian women, Enlace de Mujeres Rurales Cristianas, but is equally determined not to be put in a permanent leadership role. A number of women active in the other member organisations were a part of the original PAEM organisation, and developed their skills alongside the Macuelizo women. In María Esther's terms,

...they are trained now, they have to take it on, they have to learn. They have a methodology; they now have more ideas; they have gone through a whole process of valuing themselves, and when I started they didn't have all of that. I started with nothing... now we are at a different point. I think they are going to know how to take it on. I am going to have a power to help; it's not that I now want to know nothing... I am a part of it all, you know. But I won't do it as if I had power that I haven't. (María Esther)

The leadership model and the rigour with which it is developed, has been an essential part of the empowerment process for the PAEM women. The question of who holds power in a situation and their attitude to that power are vital issues if empowerment is to take place.

The conflict

The conflict between PAEM and Padre Ricardo, the new priest, although it resulted in the halving of the number of groups, had, in the end, a positive impact on the women who decided to stay with the programme. The fight to maintain their identity in the face of strong opposition had the effect of making the women defend themselves, articulate exactly why the programme was important to them, make their voices heard and be visible in a way that they had not had to previously. It made them assert their independence and their desire to continue taking charge of their activities. They had to analyse what the Catholic Church meant to them and where they saw themselves in relation to it, both as individuals and as groups. In addition, the women had the chance to consider what alternatives were being offered. This account from a group discussion in El Pital illustrates some of these points:

...the priests are in favour, they support us, the bishops support us, it's just him...the ones of us who have been around the longest, we have already spent a time with CARITAS and we didn't see that that moved us forward. There was a bit of training and little projects, visits around over the years, but the women's groups weren't developed like they are now. It's likely we'd be organised into those same old groups again. We saw that it was better to stay with this education programme for women, where we're receiving better training. The groups were even making presentations in big meetings, where we talked a lot about women's rights; we were taking steps forward and why would we want to take steps backwards, to return to the same old thing?

So that was our decision, and it was only our new priest who didn't accept that ... he wanted us to put ourselves under the authority of CARITAS. Well, we didn't want to return to being what they call 'the son of authority' ... And so we didn't accept it, and the priest now more or less says nothing and it's better now. ...With the conflict there's been perhaps we wouldn't be here now, because there were bad things they called us... but at the same time we knew the training we had had and we weren't going to leave the organisation   .

And also the consejo was firm right through. If the consejo had weakened perhaps all of the women would have weakened; but no, there was great resolution. ... I think that if we hadn't formed the consejo, the women's groups wouldn't exist. (El Pital group)

Many rumours were circulating about the women and the programme during the conflict. The women were under pressure to believe them, and had to do their own thinking and analysis in order to resist them. For example, it was being said that the women were being manipulated by outsiders for political ends, by implying a communist source of funding. They were able to resist this rumour:

[Oxfam] has its office in Mexico, not in Cuba like they say [laughter]. *I know it's ignorance ... It's alright, because for me Cuba isn't a monster, Cuba is human beings too and according to what I've heard on the radio, perhaps they live a thousand times [worse] than we do, and they present it as if it were a tiger, but it's not like that, when you meet with the others to study you listen to the radio and you realise that things aren't how they are presented.* (El Pital group)

During the conflict the *consejo* played a crucial role of communicating with the groups and of strategising to resist the pressures and overcome the problem. They decided that a contributing cause of the conflict was that they had not been following the usual path for work with women. María Esther said,

If we had thought, well, we'll do little projects, we wouldn't have had problems. But our concern wasn't in doing little projects, our concern was in reflecting, in reconceptualising the role of women. (María Esther)

Again according to María Esther, they were open to dialogue with the priest, the women's pastoral committee, and members of the parish council throughout the conflict, but did not achieve it:

...he resisted talking to me, because he thought that those ideas were mine but not those of the rest of the women. So we analysed it in our meeting of the consejo...I said to them, right, I have no interest, I have every faith that you all have the capacity to deal with it, and let's name a team to continue the dialogue, and I'll pull out from it. So the team carried on the dialogue, which was a monologue, really, it wasn't a dialogue; and we maintained the possibility of

co-ordinating, of mutual respect: that we belonged to the same church, that we have problems in common. So we saw the need for autonomy, that we should take our own decisions. That's where the conflict was, in the taking of decisions [A delegation went to the parish assembly in 1992] ... in the discussion they tried to humiliate them, and moreover they threw them out. It was the behaviour of politicians, not of Christians.

...they said with the whole campaign, that we wanted to order men around, that we are an organisation from outside... And on the other hand, if we take our own decisions and continue maintaining our own space, then we no longer belong to the church. In order to belong to the church we have to belong to the CARITAS programme and destroy what is the women's programme...

Then we had our assembly to analyse and to reflect on the conflict. And we agreed our watchword, that ... we won't be anyone's groups. The pattern here in Honduras is that women's groups have to be church groups or groups of some nearby masculine structure, or groups of an NGO. And we were very clear that we will not be a group of anyone because that signifies subordination, submission. So we will be Christian women and we will carry on being Christian, with all that that implies...

(María Esther: extracts from three separate interviews)

It is clear that the women on the *consejo* have been strengthened because of the experience. During the worst of the conflict they went from meeting monthly to meeting once a week, and used the time to voice doubts and express strong emotion as well as to plan and strategise. María Esther describes this:

One thing which I think saved us was that in the face of conflict we agreed to have frequent meetings. ... They allowed us to share, although they also served for crying about everything that was happening but, but at the same time to give us strength, to make new proposals, to revise proposals; and although there was much suffering, there were also successes that we wouldn't have achieved by other means. We created an atmosphere in the consejo of comradeship, of solidarity, of sisterhood that we couldn't be divided... And now we're sisters. Before, perhaps we saw the compañera who represented such and such a place; and now we love each other and we have confidence in each other... we are family. I still don't understand how it was possible in the face of such an avalanche that the group didn't divide. ... I think we came out recognising that what we can maintain is 15 groups and from here we'll move forwards. (María Esther)

Factors working against empowerment

The women I interviewed identified a number of aspects which they perceived as obstacles to their personal and group development, either currently or in the past; some of these have been touched upon earlier. They talked about problems in their relationships with their husbands or families and the strong culture of *machismo*. They also talked about the levels of dependency fostered by relationships with development agencies and other organisations which organise on the basis of donated food or small projects — and the demoralising effect of having such projects fail or be withdrawn.

They see poverty as their lot, and have a fatalistic attitude to many things, which has to be overcome every time they decide to act. They see that practical and tangible difficulties also impede the empowerment process. For example, Alicia refers to the issues of leaving the house untended and of childcare:

I haven't wanted to [be an animator for the group] up to now partly because of the little boy.

Q: *But once he's bigger you might?*

A: *Bigger, yes, although there's another thing ... you have to find someone to look after the house for you. You'd have to pay someone, and the groups don't have the money... so what can you do? You can't just leave the house. They've told me to go on the animators' course, but this is why I haven't wanted to, with the young one it's difficult.* (Alicia, 31, El Pital)

This appears to be a particular issue for younger women. Most of the animators are women who have older children who can care for the younger ones and mind the house, and are therefore in their mid-thirties or older. Some groups have members who have young children and who bring them with them to meetings; but they tend to be more passive in their participation. Women who have no means of divesting themselves of any part of their child care or other domestic responsibilities have little time available to invest in other activities.

Women talked constantly about their roles as wives, mothers, and housewives, which they saw as inevitable ones for women. Very few of them talked about any role as active providers of livelihood or as workers. When asked what they thought life would be like for their daughters, most of them expected it to be similar to their own (though 'hopefully she'll find a better man and won't have the troubles I've had' was a common rider to the reply). A few expected their daughters to find work in the *maquila*. It seems that in order to empower themselves, these women will need to free themselves further from the inflexibilities of what it is to them to be a woman. Some of them were also talking of their plans for the warehouse project, assuming they would be fully involved in it, so it is not that they do not see themselves as able to move into new areas of influence. Internalised oppression is firmly embedded in their psyches, and is constantly being reinforced by the expectations of other people and society as a whole. Although able to make decisions and act, despite that internalised oppression, women are inhibited by it in the process of becoming empowered, and it conditions the way they think about themselves. Also, in a situation where women's hopes may have been raised and dashed many times, it is understandable that there will be reticence and caution.

Another important issue was the use and control of land. Many of the PAEM groups have taken on small agricultural projects, usually on land lent by a *grupo campesino*. These projects have usually failed, often because the land is unsuitable (perhaps being too far away from the village), or because it is reclaimed from the women once it becomes productive. Another common problem with these projects has been crop failure, which may be due to the women's inexperience, and also to the lack of appropriate technical support.

A lack of appropriate technical support also affects the work of PAEM as a whole, now that they have started on a project that will meet some of their needs for income and a reliable supply of basic grain, as María Esther identifies, in the context of the warehouse project :

we need technical support because we can't do what we want to do alone...
but we haven't found a qualified technical advisor with gender awareness, with
awareness of the problems that poor women face. Maybe there is someone like
that in the country, but we haven't found them; we're bothered because it seems
to be out of our reach. (María Esther)

This problem was partly about finding technical support that is 'neutral' and will not make them dependent on an NGO or government body with a different perspective and agenda. When I first arrived, a female technical advisor was working with the *consejo* to assess the feasibility of the warehouse project. She could only work with them for two sessions, however, whilst between jobs. By the time I left they had not found a replacement. There was less concern about finding help to learn the practical skills of running a warehouse, since through María Esther's husband they have contact with a successful warehouse project in Yoro.

Other factors inhibiting the process of empowerment lie in the context and socio-political history of the area. *Caudillismo* is still a strong force in Honduras. This means that powerful individuals, while they can help the empowerment process, as in the case of PAEM, can also work against it, because individuals rely on the leader to the detriment of their own development. Choosing *animadoras* from within the groups, and the *consejo* structure, minimise this effect, but it is nonetheless a dynamic that continues to operate within the groups. It is also imposed from the outside, with people often referring to PAEM as 'María Esther's groups', and assuming she makes all the decisions. María Esther was herself raised within this culture of *caudillismo*; although she has a strong personal commitment to the empowerment of women and to work for the ending of *caudillismo* as a political and social force, her confidence and articulateness, her network of contacts, and her astute political analysis to some extent reinforce the *caudillo* style, since they interact with the habits of deference to strong leaders ingrained in the PAEM participants.

The nature of the local community and the political make-up of the area also affects the empowerment process. This can be see in the contrast between the communities of El Pital and Quitasueño. In El Pital, where the community is long established and there are many long-term residents and a well-developed community identity backed up by effective community organisations, the PAEM groups have flourished. Women in the groups are animated, optimistic, and active, and the groups have won support and influence in local organisations. By contrast, the one PAEM group in Quitasueño has remained small and has not taken on a strong public identity; meetings are much more subdued, although the animators are lively and optimistic. Quitasueño, as described earlier, is a recently established community, almost entirely made up of migrants from other parts of the department or from further afield. There is a history of much organisational activity, both by peasant organisations and NGOs, but with an atmosphere of manipulation, of conflict, and of competition for limited economic and political resources rather than co-operation. More women in Quitasueño than in El Pital told me of having to contend with husbands who are violent, who drink a lot, or who are womanisers. The women in the PAEM group have received little encouragement from the community, and there is local suspicion about what they are trying to achieve. That the group has survived so long in an atmosphere of suspicion and negative judgement is perhaps an indication that the women have achieved some measure of empowerment. The *animadoras*, who participate in the *consejo* meetings, are influenced by the encouragement and optimism of other women, and have opportunities to develop a wider perspective, which the other group members have not. A local culture of negativity and suspicion, and an unstable and *machista* local political climate, can have the effect of inhibiting the empowerment process for women.

Figure 5.4: Extracts from *Conociéndome a mí misma*

[The text is divided into short readings, and illustrated with photographs and drawings. The separate booklet *Guía de la Animadora* (animator's guide) provides a structure for meetings, with suggestions for small group activities, questions for discussion and some bible readings to accompany the main text.]

If I don't know who I am, if I don't know what my qualities, my capabilities and my strengths are, neither do I know my weaknesses, I don't value myself for what I am, I don't respect myself, I don't love myself. I need to know myself in order to grow and to develop as a person. If I know myself better I will be able to help others and help myself. (p. 5)

An important step in the development of our minds was when we started to distinguish good from bad. As we grew older we discovered that in this world there are good things, things that are not so bad, things that are more or less good and bad. And when we were going to do something we could now tell if there was something good or bad about what we were going to do. Sometimes we weren't sure, but as the years passed we knew more and more things. Who gave us this knowledge of good and bad, and of all the things we learned? Our parents, teachers, aunts, granny, the priest.

We also learned through our own experience. What our parents, teachers and elders were putting into our minds through their words and actions are like seeds planted in our brain. Some of these seeds are of good, prime quality. Others are of middling quality, with some defects. And some seeds are useless. (p. 20–1)

...what we must keep in our mind and our heart is this truth: God has given us a marvellous gift, a mind to think with; and if we like we can use it for our benefit and for the well-being of the community. (p. 29)

In the previous theme we saw that many men and women have used their minds, thinking and reflecting, in order to discover new ways of doing things. Some of us said we had never used our minds to do anything new or better. Many of us women think we are idiots and aren't any good for anything. Why? ... Since we were little we have been told over and over we are stupid. ... Sometimes we make mistakes when we do things because we are scared. We are scared of our parents, teachers, those with authority and those we think know more than we do. Fear gets in our way, sends our mind to sleep. Fear doesn't let us think well. So we do things wrong. It is fear that makes us make mistakes; it's not because we are stupid. ... The third reason why we seem stupid sometimes is because our mind lacks exercise. If we tie up an arm and don't move it for a month, when we get it back it will be weak, we won't be able to even lift a spoon, even less carry the baby. ... The same happens with our brain, with our mind when we don't use it to think about how to make the housework easier, to educate our children, to participate more in the meetings of the group and look for solutions to our problems. ...if we think and reflect, our mind wakes up as we brush off the cobwebs. Perhaps at first it's difficult and we have to work at it. But as the saying goes, all good things have a price. So let's get going on conquering fear and laziness. (p33–6).

Sometimes, although we are adult women and have many years of thinking behind us, we don't understand our feelings very well. We think that it's not important to dedicate time and effort to understanding them better. But many, many of the things we do are moved by some kind of feeling. Let's have an example: They invite us to be co-ordinator or animator of a group. It's work we don't know, it's a new responsibility. So we say *I can't. I've got so much to do at home. I have four young ones and one is still breastfeeding. I can't accept. Because if I did it wouldn't go well, for you or for my family.* What this woman is saying is true. She has many obligations at home. She is right in part, to say she can't accept the responsibility of co-ordinator or animator. Why say she is right in part? Because in her soul she has a feeling which is pushing her to say *I can't.* What is that feeling? She feels fear, fear of what she doesn't know, fear of doing badly, fear of getting it wrong. It's true that she has a lot to do, but it's the same for other women who have accepted the responsibility. If we don't understand our feelings we can make wrong decisions. We can also delude ourselves. On the other hand, if we understand our feelings better we can rule our lives better and give our children better guidance. (p. 60–2).

If someone lacks respect for us, if someone betrays us or treats us badly, it's normal to feel sadness, discouragement, anger or fear. Moreover if, since we were girls at home, we have received little love, little affection, and we were not respected, now we are grown up mistreatment or betrayal hurts us a lot. And it almost always costs us much effort to treat our children, others and ourselves, with respect, with justice. (p. 68–9).

We have seen that many of us have the same problems. For example, in our village there is no water, no light, no adequate school, no land to work, no employment, no health centre or medicines or nurses and food is scarcer and more expensive every day. All this is an injustice that makes us feel bad. But if because of this situation we keep complaining and spending time in talk, making ourselves victims, we are like the cat which chases its own tail. We go round in circles and do nothing But if we see these injustices and feel angry, that's good, so long as we do not take it out on our children. This anger should make us look for possible solutions. Because most other women in the country have the problems we have. We need to stop being individualistic; we need to join with other women who have the same problems and interests. (p. 76–7).

6

Analysing empowerment: a dynamic view

Let us now return to the issue of 'empowerment': what it is and how it might be cultivated. The simple model of three dimensions of empowerment, described in chapter 2, while a useful approach, is not adequate for detailed analysis. While it emphasises the different contexts in which empowerment can be experienced and exercised (at a personal level, in relationships, and within a group), it does not fully represent the interactions between them, does not give details of what empowerment consists of, and does not distinguish between 'processes' and 'changes that may occur because of those processes'. It is inadequate for discussion of the operation of power in a specific context, or of the different forms of power. I found that it failed to represent the complexity of empowerment processes as they occurred in either of the case-study organisations. In addition to these shortcomings, the model does not provide sufficient analytical capacity to make it useful to an external agency looking to identify appropriate interventions.

Empowerment processes involve a complex inter-relation and interaction between a multitude of different elements; and those inter-relations and interactions are dynamic. For example, increased economic independence may contribute to an increase in individual self-confidence; or increased individual self-confidence may contribute to an increase in economic independence. Indeed, the two may relate to each other in a circular manner that makes it difficult to differentiate between them. In order to separate out the elements and to show how they interact, a more dynamic, more fluid model is needed.

The various aspects of empowerment can be categorised into three groups: 'contextual', or 'material', being part of the environment in some way; 'structural', in terms of the nature of the organisations and their activities; and 'inner' psychological or psycho-social processes. This latter category seems to be most consistent, both between the two case studies and across interviews. Most outside observers referred to aspects in this category as being the most significant area of change they perceived. Involving self-perception and the undoing of 'internalised oppression', this category appears to be central to processes of empowerment.

We can thus distinguish between the 'core' of the empowerment process, that is, the transformation of the individual or the group that is the 'key' that opens 'locks' on the empowerment door; and the circumstances that appear to encourage or inhibit the process.

The individual or group brings to the process of empowerment an existing experience and history. The process does not suddenly start (or finish) at a certain point in time, but has been operating in various ways ever since the group existed or the individual was born. Prior experience can affect the empowerment process in a variety of ways; it may affect the strength of particular encouraging or inhibiting pressures; it may 'bias' the areas in which new power is gained. For example, a woman with scarcely any experience of interacting with people outside her immediate family may be developing her self-confidence and self-esteem in terms of her capacity to engage with her peers and with new situations close to home. A woman with experience of some sort of leadership will also be developing self-confidence and self-esteem, but for her these processes are likely to be manifested in her interactions with more experienced leaders, with authority or with organisational tasks which 'stretch' her in some way. The way in which the two women respond to inhibiting factors, such as demands on their time, will be different. The woman with experience of leadership will almost certainly have coped with such constraints in other situations, and have developed strategies to deal with them.

Let us now develop this new model with reference to the case studies, using material from interviews and conversations with the women involved.

Personal empowerment

The 'core'

The 'core' of the empowerment process involves fundamental psychological and psycho-social processes and changes, to which individual women alluded repeatedly. Central to these are the development of self-confidence and self-esteem, and a sense of agency, of being an individual who can interact with her surroundings and cause things to happen. I would also include 'dignity' in the core aspects. This

Figure 4 PAEM: Personal empowerment

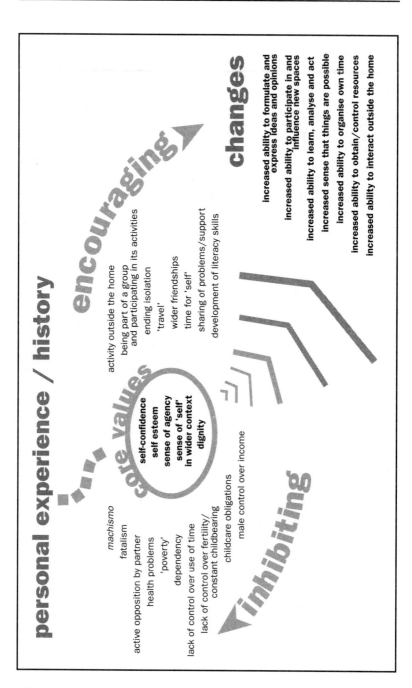

is a word many of my interviewees used, to mean self-respect, self-esteem, and a sense of being not only worthy of respect from others, but of having a right to that respect. I have also included 'a sense of self within a wider context'. Although not as explicitly identified in interviews, it seems to be an essential part of the 'core' if the individual is to be able to move out of the gender-assigned roles that her context and culture have given her.[1]

In Urraco, the development of self-confidence and self-esteem were very clearly identified, and were seen as the main areas of change achieved by women participating in the programme. Other core elements, such as a sense of self in a wider context, sense of agency, and dignity are also discernible. In PAEM all the core elements were strongly present.

Encouraging factors

Urraco interviewees described the isolation they had experienced prior to the programme as a severe limitation on their lives. They identified a number of ways in which their activity in the health programme helped them to break that isolation. These included getting out of the house and out of the immediate community, making friends, and participating in group activities. Learning health-related and literacy skills contributed to the development of their confidence. Other 'encouraging' elements identified were the issuing of diplomas on completion of the two-year course, the chance to share problems and get support, and the encouragement of the US volunteer and the parish priest. The programme gave them a role in the community which carries prestige. Some of the women identified the fact of the programme working only with women as a feature that helped to build their confidence.

PAEM interviewees identified a number of features of the PAEM programme which contributed to the core of the empowerment process. Travel, activity outside the home, sharing of problems and group activities, reduce the isolation of the individual woman in her home and immediate family, and give her wider opportunities for interaction. The individual has the chance to develop particular skills, both practical (such as literacy) and social (participation in meetings and discussions). Many features of the programme have the effect of strengthening the identity of the individual, apart from her role as housewife and mother, and helping her to focus not only on the needs of others but also on her own needs.[2] This makes it easier for the individual to generate ideas and hold opinions that differ from those of other people, which is a necessary ability for exercising power. The spiritual base of the programme was also seen as important, as was the opportunity to express strong emotions.

Inhibiting factors

The women also identified obstacles to the empowerment process. In Urraco, many such inhibiting factors are components of the cultural, social, and physical conditions in which the women live, and the gender roles to which they are expected to conform. These include *machismo*, with their husbands not giving permission to participate, and negative stereotypes and gossip in the wider community about women who participate. There are economic and political obstacles as well: the lack of employment opportunities in the area, the tendency of the men to control family income, the impunity enjoyed by men who use violence against women. Women lack control over their own fertility, and have child-care obligations which make it difficult to participate in the programme. Other obstacles are linked to the structure of the programme itself. The 'course' format provides a built-in 'end' to women's involvement, and gives a rather static picture of what can and should be achieved. A relationship is constructed between people who have knowledge and others who do not, which restricts individual or group initiative. In addition, the role of the study-circle co-ordinators is a limited one, and there are few opportunities for them to develop their abilities. The 'course' structure also encourages dependency of the groups on members of the co-ordinating team.

For the women involved in PAEM, many of the elements inhibiting empowerment are the same, arising from the cultural, social, and physical context, or the political and economic situation these women face. For the women in both programmes, the obstacles to empowerment include elements of the oppression under which they live, both as females and as poor people, and of the 'internalised oppression' with which they have to engage if they wish to change their situation and position. The development of the 'core' of the empowerment process for the individual women in Urraco and PAEM has been successful (or unsuccessful), therefore, to the extent that they have been able individually to overcome the effects of the inhibiting factors, using the strengths they gain from the encouraging factors, building on their individual experience and history.

Personal empowerment and change

The process of empowerment is both experienced as a feeling of personal change and development, and also manifested, or demonstrated, in changed behaviour. Each woman experiences the process in an individual way, related to her own history, circumstances, and actions.

Some of the changes linked with personal empowerment in Urraco are quite specific, including the learning of particular skills (such as those needed to run the *botiquínes* and the weighing sessions); for a few women this has led to employment. Less tangible, but nonetheless evident, are an increased ability to interact outside the home, a sense of having the ability to choose responses, and of being able to participate in activities in a way that they would not have been able to do before. There is also an increased ability to participate in the small groups and in the larger sectoral meetings (including in other fora such as the church), and for some, a sense of value and therefore an expectation of being paid for their work.

The changes most often referred to by the PAEM women interviewed include an increased ability to formulate and express ideas and opinions, and to participate in and influence new areas of activity; to learn, analyse, and act. They have a sense that more things are possible, and this brings an increased ability to organise their time, obtain resources, and interact outside the home.

Collective empowerment

The 'collective empowerment' dimension is very closely related to the personal dimension, since without empowerment at a personal level it is very hard for the individual to be active collectively. It is likewise very difficult for a group to become active and effective without some critical mass of individuals participating who have achieved a degree of personal empowerment. There is also a circular interrelationship: participation in the group may feed the process of personal empowerment, and vice versa. The process of collective empowerment builds on any pre-existing experience of individual members of the group of participation in other groups or collective activities.

For the purposes of our analysis, we need to identify the elements of empowerment experienced by group members *by virtue of their membership of the group*; and to consider 'the group' as if it were a separate entity, distinct from its members. Although this is an artificial distinction — clearly, only individuals can have, for example, a 'sense of self' or 'agency' — it enables us to make illuminating comparisons between personal and collective empowerment processes.

The 'core'

The 'core' of collective empowerment in Urraco was very different for the Health Promoters and for the co-ordinating team members. The Health Promoters told me that their confidence in themselves, as a group, has increased somewhat. A few of the study circles had organised

Figure 5 PAEM: Collective Empowerment

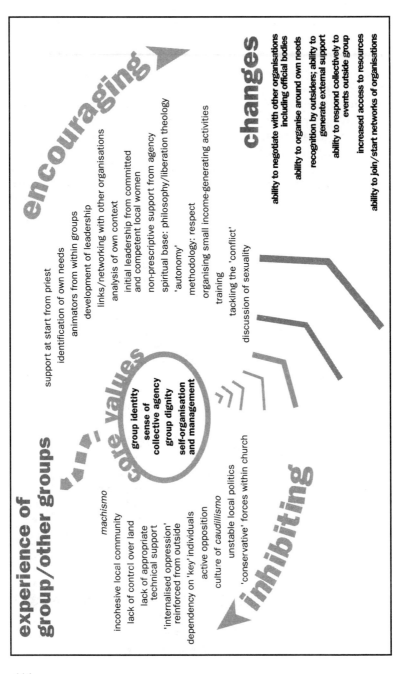

other activities in addition to studying, so we can include a 'sense of collective agency' and 'self-organisation and management' in the 'core' for the Health Promoters. For the members of the co-ordinating team the picture is much more definite. They have developed a sense of identity and dignity as a team, and have taken on 'ownership' of the programme to a large extent. There is evidence of the development of a group 'sense of agency', particularly in the way they were responding to the impending withdrawal of funding, and preparing to take over the management of the programme. In PAEM, the 'core' of collective empowerment is analogous to that of personal empowerment, focusing on group identity, dignity, and agency.

Self-organisation and management could be seen either as a core element of empowerment or as a change in behaviour by which empowerment is demonstrated. However, for our purposes, it is appropriate to categorise it as a core element, because it is both connected with and reinforcing of other core elements. So often in development projects with women's groups where self-organisation and management have not been encouraged, external politics or the withdrawal of external support have resulted in the collapse of the group.

Encouraging factors

For the Urraco Health Promoters, the development of group confidence has been encouraged by the various ways in which groups have interacted. The support of the priest has also been a positive influence. The groups have developed status and identity within the communities, particularly through the weighing sessions.

There are many features encouraging the development of the 'core' of collective empowerment in PAEM. Some of them are related to the organisational form used: the emphasis on developing leadership from within the groups and on training, the methodology based on respect and learning from experience. Others are related to the activities undertaken, including small income-generating projects, and networking. Encouragement has also taken the form of support from key individuals such as the priest and the funding agency. María Esther also encouraged the self-confidence and autonomy of groups. Other encouraging features are the commitment to empowerment implicit in the philosophy and methodology of PAEM, which has some of its origins in liberation theology; and the 'autonomy' developed by the programme over time. Surviving the conflict with the new priest also strengthened collective empowerment.

Inhibiting factors

The 'inhibiting' features identified in relation to the Urraco Health Promoters include some related to the social and cultural conditions, such as the strong 'donation culture' and attitude of dependency. Economic obstacles, particularly related to the system of land tenure and the large-scale export-oriented agriculture of the area, discourage the groups from tackling collective projects. Other obstacles relate to the structure of the programme itself, including the lack of autonomous activities for groups, and the focus on individual learning. The programme does not provide a sense of creating something together. The dependency on the co-ordinating team also inhibits collective empowerment.

For the Urraco co-ordinating team, the obstacles to collective empowerment include some of the cultural and social elements previously identified. The economics of the region, with the dominant focus on large-scale monoculture for export, also diminish the team's sense of its ability to act.

The elements inhibiting the development of collective empowerment in PAEM also include cultural characteristics, in terms of *machismo* and *caudillismo*, both reinforced by the action of conservative forces within the church. Other elements, such as the fragmented local community and unstable local politics in the case of Quitasueño, lack of control over land, and lack of appropriate technical support, are related to the local or national political and economic context or more generally to the situation of women in relation to the law. Another obstacle to collective empowerment has been dependency on key individuals, and (paradoxically, given her largely positive role) on María Esther in particular.

Collective empowerment changes

For the Urraco Health Promoters, there is little evidence of collective empowerment leading to action. However, the Urraco co-ordinating team have started to meet regularly with the Literacy team, for mutual support and to devise a fundraising strategy. The co-ordinating team has gradually taken over all the management of the health programme, and had developed their own links with national and international networks. They were also active in organising lobbying and protest in relation to the murder of Nelly Suazo and the impunity of her killer, and these activities brought the team (plus Nelly's own study circle) a reinforced sense of collective purpose and determination.

Changes resulting from collective empowerment include an ability to negotiate with other organisations, including official bodies. PAEM now has recognition from outsiders and an ability to generate external support for its activities. The women are now able to organise collectively to meet their own needs, to respond together to events outside the group, and to join and initiate networks of organisations. Their ability to obtain resources, such as funding, expertise, and equipment, has increased.

Empowerment within close relationships

The 'core'

To have a sense of empowerment in relation to other people, is associated with, and to a large extent, dependent upon, self-confidence, self-esteem, and sense of agency. It also depends on the development of the individual's abilities to negotiate, communicate, and defend his or her rights (overtly or covertly). Such skills themselves also represent 'changes' demonstrating personal empowerment.

Encouraging and inhibiting factors and changes

The women in the Urraco Health Programme did not talk much to me about their close relationships and there was much less consistency in their experience. (This partly reflects the higher proportion of single women in the programme.) The 'core' elements they identified related to the abilities to negotiate and communicate. Obviously, if their partner was supportive, this represented an 'encouraging' element, and the women experienced a greater sense of empowerment in their relationship with him. The factors inhibiting empowerment were related to the culture of *machismo*, alcohol consumption, and other *vicios* (vices), and the strong culture of violence. They were experienced very strongly by the women closest to Nelly Suazo, when she was murdered. That represented a clear and powerful message as to what can happen to a woman who 'pushes too hard' for change in her relationships, and who encourages and supports others to do the same. Changes demonstrating empowerment included more talking with husbands, an increased involvement in domestic decision-making, and more co-operative relationships with neighbours.

The women in PAEM felt that empowerment in close relationships was encouraged by their participation in the groups and by the ending of their individual isolation in their homes; in particular, the opportunity to share problems with other women was seen as important. It has made a big difference to them to have a concept of 'women's rights' and a knowledge of what those rights might consist of, and a perception of inequalities in relationships between people as wrong. The forces

Figure 6 PAEM: Empowerment within close relationships

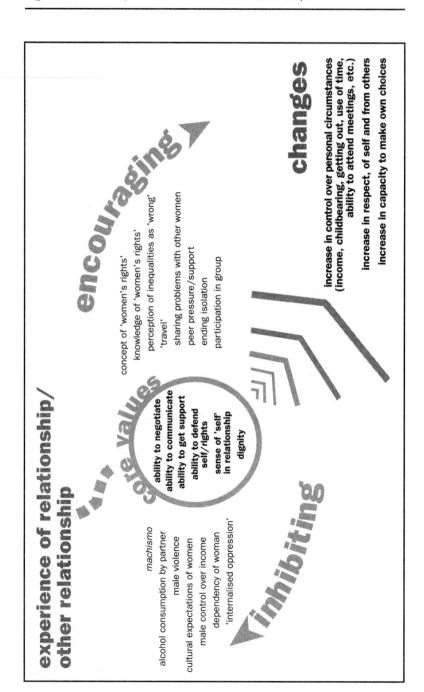

working against empowerment in close relationships, in addition to general cultural factors, included the economic dependency of most women. Men usually controlled income and other resources. 'Internalised oppression' is a major obstacle to empowerment here, reinforcing any actual dependency. For women who have achieved positive change in their personal relationships, whether with husbands or other close relatives including mothers-in-law, the 'changes' include an increase in control over their personal circumstances (income, fertility, use of time, and ability to attend meetings). They also describe an increase in respect from others, including their husbands.

Urraco and PAEM compared

Looking at the overall picture, in the case of the Urraco Health Programme, the programme has achieved a measure of empowerment with the Health Promoters, in the form of personal empowerment, which has opened up their horizons and given them opportunities for social interactions and, for some, to new economic possibilities. Some of them have been empowered to make changes in their relationships. The programme has had a more marked impact on women in the co-ordinating team, in terms of personal empowerment, in some of their close relationships, and in their ability to act collectively. My research on PAEM gave a picture of significant empowerment for women throughout the organisation, in terms of personal and collective empowerment, although empowerment is less clearly demonstrated within close relationships.

Can this model of empowerment help to explain the areas of difference between the two case studies, and to strengthen the analysis not just in terms of its structure, but in its content, which could then be tested in other contexts?

Personal empowerment

The common elements which form the core of personal empowerment in each case study, are the development of individual self-confidence and self-esteem, coupled with a sense of self in a wider context (though I would say that this latter is on the whole less developed in the Urraco women). In PAEM, there is also the development of a sense of individual agency and 'dignity'. Turning to the 'encouraging' features, many are broadly similar between the two groups, though the Urraco list is longer. Some of those extra elements (the women-only nature of the group, the sense of having a role in the community, and the support of the priest) were also present in PAEM (in the case of support of the priest, at least initially) though they were not identified in interviews. In PAEM spirituality is specifically mentioned whereas in Urraco it is not. Likewise with the inhibiting features: there is broad similarity, with some elements identified in one case appearing to apply in the other even if not referred to by those interviewed.

The main area of difference is the structural features of the two programmes. In Urraco these are identified as inhibiting empowerment, whereas in PAEM the structural features of the programme are 'encouraging'. It is in considering the 'changes' by which personal empowerment is demonstrated that a marked difference becomes apparent between the two case studies. In PAEM, the 'changes' could be seen as the result of the development of general communication and analytical skills, which are the skills necessary for interaction with wider society. While not necessarily increasing the individual's ability to use 'power over', they are strongly related to the exercise of 'power to': generative power, the power to create and participate in new forms of activity. They are also skills that can be used for resistance. These changes at a personal level affect collective empowerment: with more ability to formulate and express opinions, a woman can take a more active role in group and economic activities, and in her interactions with other members of the community; with more control over her use of time she can participate more actively and on revised terms in group activities or in other activities in the family or the community, and so on. There is also a circular 'feedback' effect, in that the acquisition of new skills reinforces the development of self-confidence and self-esteem.

Women in Urraco were noticeably less articulate about changes they had experienced as a result of their involvement with the programme. The changes are much more limited in scope than those experienced by the PAEM women, and less effective in terms of 'widening of options' or 'ability to exercise power' through developing analysis and taking action. The co-ordinating team seemed to me to have developed more of these 'changes' than they were aware of. The Urraco 'changes' are more oriented to specific skills, and are far less flexible than those of PAEM, related as they are to access to power within a limited sphere.

So why the difference? Two explanations are suggested by differences in the 'core' elements. First, that the elements of agency and *dignidad* may be crucial aspects of empowerment, and that without them the overall effect is weakened. Second, that the structural differences between the two programmes encouraged different processes of empowerment. The PAEM structure encouraged women to practise the skills of analysis, for example, whereas the Health Promoter programme shared knowledge based on pre-existing analysis by outsiders. The focus of both programmes on non-economic activities reveals another difference. In the case of PAEM, this is a factor which supports the empowerment process. In Urraco, the non-economic focus was within the setting of a programme with considerable economic costs and very little potential for generating resources. In PAEM, the non-economic focus was a crucial part of the methodology, but used in a way that opened up a wide range of possibilities for economic empowerment, related to social empowerment. This indicates that the most important aspects of programmes and activities intended to encourage empowerment are the forms of organisation and the development of organisational strength and agency, built on the foundations of individual agency.

Collective empowerment

The process of collective empowerment is very different for the Health Promoters in Urraco, for the Urraco co-ordinating team, and for the PAEM women. While the study-circles have developed some self-confidence as groups, they seem to have no sense of group agency. Although the Health Promoters identified a number of features of the programme that might be seen as encouraging collective empowerment, it is not a long list and overlaps significantly with the equivalent list for personal empowerment. The list of factors seen as inhibiting is much longer. Some are cultural and social, but many relate to the structure of the programme itself.

The Urraco co-ordinating team and the PAEM women share the same 'core' elements for collective empowerment, i.e. group identity, a sense of collective agency, group dignity, and self-organisation and management. From my observations of both groups, these elements are more developed in the PAEM women. For example, the Urraco team were managing their programme within the form and scope already established, whereas the PAEM women were managing a constantly changing agenda and adapting to new possibilities as they arose. The 'encouraging' elements have some similarities, but also differences: in PAEM, there is a greater emphasis on deliberate development of leadership capacity, and the organisation of activities by the local groups. The PAEM methodology, which involves analysis and understanding, and the encouragement of leaders from within the groups, was developed in order to counter the influence of inhibiting factors, notably, 'internalised oppression'. Other aspects, though less deliberate, had the same effect, such as the way in which the organisation handled the conflict with the new priest and his supporters. In Urraco the elements encouraging collective empowerment for the co-ordinating team were not structurally embedded in the programme and were more dependent on circumstances.

In PAEM, the changes connected with collective empowerment reinforce the development of the core aspects as well as resulting from them. These 'changes' also reflect an increase in 'power to', both in terms of the activities that become possible and in terms of influence. 'Power to' can also be seen in the setting up of a network of *campesina* women's organisations at a national level. In beginning to relate to government and other national (and international) bodies, PAEM has also apparently gained some 'power over'. This can be seen, for example, in the assignment of the disused grain warehouse to PAEM in the face of strong opposition from the local *grupos campesinos* and the CNTC. In the changes related to collective empowerment, then, the PAEM women have developed a set of skills that have wider possibilities and have set their own goals outside of the original framework of the programme.

In contrast, the Urraco women have taken power in relation to their own programme but have stayed broadly within the pre-defined framework. There is no doubt that they see it as their task to find the funding they need, and that they are determined to achieve self-sufficiency, although there was no certainty that the activities they were planning would raise adequate funds.[3] They were focused on keeping the programme functioning, but there was no indication that they were thinking about tackling other issues and broadening their range of influence. It is interesting that the PAEM programme is maintained now wholly by voluntary input, from group members and from *consejo* members, whereas in Urraco the co-ordinating team are all paid for their work, and the Health Promoters are not.

Self-organisation and management are features that make PAEM in particular stand out from many other women's 'projects'. The PAEM groups vary somewhat in their level of collective empowerment, but the organisation as a whole has achieved a strong identity and sense of agency, with the organisation and management of PAEM activities in the hands of a team of members from the various groups. María Esther Ruiz is strongly committed to ensuring that the women are able to maintain the programme whether or not she is involved.

Close relationships

Empowerment within close relationships, in both the case studies, is seen to depend on developing the skills of negotiation and communication. For women in PAEM, these skills are made far more effective by the ability to defend rights within a relationship. The PAEM women were clear that their concept of 'women's rights' affected the nature of their personal relationships. They believed that inequalities and domination in relationships are wrong. In Urraco, although women had talked to me about women's rights in other contexts, they did not identify their knowledge of the subject as relevant to their intimate relationships.

Looking at the 'inhibiting' elements, in PAEM the women considered that men's control over income, and women's consequent dependency, was getting in their way — an understanding that the Urraco women did not seem to have reached. The 'changes' in the PAEM case reflect the more active and self-defending attitude, with, for at least some of the women, a marked change in their control over their circumstances and their ability to make choices. In Urraco these changes are scarcely detectable. I think it is significant that, whereas PAEM had involved the partners of women in some of its activities, and had, for example, sought active support from the men at the time of the conflict with the priest, this was not the case in Urraco (although Monica and the co-ordinating team had identified the need, and a very small number of men had come to a few meetings). I had very little success in interviewing husbands of the women I interviewed in Urraco, in order to get their perspective, whereas in El Pital, and somewhat less so in Quitasueño, the men were very happy to be interviewed and to share their thinking on what had been achieved by the women.

Empowerment within the context of close relationships does not appear to be an invariable consequence of personal empowerment. In many respects, to make changes within relationships seem to be the most difficult area of change for women. Some of the individual women who are playing the most active roles in PAEM, as animators and as members of the *consejo*, have major difficulties in their relationships with their partners, and some perceive those relationships as something they will never be able to do anything about. This is probably because a woman receives support and encouragement from others in relation to her personal empowerment, but in attempting to change a relationship with her partner she is much more isolated. In a group one woman can be carried along with others. On her own, she has to use her own resources.

In addition, close relationships may be characterised by great ambiguity: they can be the location of support and caring as well as struggle and disempowerment. In taking risks to challenge the latter, the former may be put in jeopardy. Empowerment in this dimension not only involves changes in the woman's own expectations and behaviour, but also changes in the expectations and behaviour of her partner and close family members. Where the women have succeeded in making changes in their close relationships, these can have a marked impact on other aspects of their lives. Some women have achieved major transformations in their close relationships; others have made smaller changes that nonetheless enable them to participate more freely in the group or to make a few more decisions for themselves.

Summary of comparison

It would appear that the structure of the PAEM programme has equipped the women participants with a wider range of options than they had before, particularly in relation to collective empowerment. In comparison, the impact of the Urraco programme has been patchy, perhaps because the only specific focus on empowerment came from the individual US volunteer. The programme was not conceived and designed to facilitate the empowerment of women, in terms of either the structure and methodology, or of the philosophy behind it. The focus has been strongly on delivering a particular service through developing the necessary skills, rather than a more general development of broad abilities and capacities which would leave women better placed to address their problems as they themselves defined them.

Power within the empowerment process

What kinds of power are being generated in the change processes described above? Does the analysis throw any light on the nature of power being exercised in the empowerment of the case-study groups? Increases in self-esteem and self-confidence change the nature of the interaction between the individuals or groups and the environment; an increased sense of agency increases the possibility of acting in the world, of making changes. Having a sense of self in relation to a wider context than before broadens the field within which action is likely to happen. It seems, therefore, that the core qualities are those necessary for the exercise of 'power-to' or 'power-with'. 'Power-from-within' is also represented in the form of dignity, which rests on an inner strength.

It is in the 'changes' seen in the two organisations that the operation of power becomes more visible, particularly where women move into new activities or new positions within the community. Most of the 'changes' seen in Urraco and PAEM are examples of 'power-to' and 'power with'; for instance, the ability to respond collectively to events outside the group. It is possible, also, for 'power-over' to be exercised; for example, an increased ability to learn, analyse, and act could be used by an individual to dominate a group and prioritise their own agenda. This is less likely to happen where these abilities are developed in an atmosphere that prioritises 'power-with'. So, for example, it was PAEM as a group, rather than an individual woman in PAEM, that negotiated to operate the grain warehouse.

'Power-to' and 'power-with' can be seen also in the factors encouraging the empowerment process. Some of these focus on the acquisition of knowledge, and the expansion of opportunities. Support from a priest or external development agency, are examples of the use of 'power with' to encourage a group to develop 'power to'. 'Power-over' is most visible in the inhibiting elements, such as *machismo*, male violence, and women's lack of control over their fertility or over land; it is present in a very negative form, as power that obstructs women's empowerment.

The analysis of power and its exercise *within* processes of empowerment could be taken much further than this simple outline. It raises further questions about means and ends. For example, what kind of power should an influential person involved in the empowerment of an individual or group use to promote a particular kind of Monica in Urraco and María Esther in PAEM each encouraged and supported groups of women; did their different situations (Monica as a woman from the United States, with all that that implies in relation to Honduras; and María Esther as a local *campesina*) mean that they had a different range of possible forms of power available to them? Did they use power differently in their work with the groups? Or, as a further example, the three priests mentioned in the two case studies were all significant in relation to empowerment processes. What kinds of power did they each use in relation to the case-study organisations? Did that make a difference to the impacts that they had on the groups? In the PAEM case, both priests were members of the same Passionist order; both were men from peninsular Spain. One was very supportive, the other was not. Did the fact that Jesús María was from the Basque country influence his exercise of power in relation to the groups?

Conclusion

The model shows clearly that it is not enough to take the 'core' in any one dimension and say 'this is what empowerment consists of'; for example, having more self-confidence and dignity do not necessarily lead to changes in how power is exercised or experienced. It is the action that arises from the core qualities which is significant. In other words, empowerment cannot simply be equated with self-confidence and dignity; it is also what happens *as a result* of having self-confidence and dignity. Hence the need for 'a sense of agency' as an essential element of personal or collective empowerment. Empowerment processes are dynamic, and the three dimensions of empowerment suggested in the model are closely linked: positive changes in one dimension can encourage changes in either the same dimension or in another. Factors which encourage empowerment can be reinforced and are reinforcing; inhibiting factors and obstacles can be mitigated, and overcome, thus serving to encourage and affirm empowerment.

The account of empowerment I have developed here has been based on observations of two specific organisations. Generalisations on the subject should only be drawn tentatively and cautiously, especially given the importance of context; any organisation, project or programme will have its own unique circumstances and history, and operate within a particular cultural environment. However, I have attempted to provide a structure and some indicators for evaluating empowerment processes, and an analysis which is neither static nor culture-bound. It is clear that empowerment takes many forms, and any analysis therefore cannot hope to be definitive; I offer it here as a contribution to ongoing discussion. The analysis of power and its exercise *within* processes of empowerment adds a further dimension of complexity to the debate.

A comparison with the accounts of other writers on empowerment is useful for highlighting similarities and differences between their conclusions and my own. For example, Kabeer also emphasises the importance of such elements as self-respect and a sense of agency to empowerment processes; the way in which the collective dimension of empowerment can be an adjunct to personal empowerment; and the significance of methodology and organisational processes. Batliwala's account of empowerment recognises the importance of psychological as well as material processes, and she is also clear that empowerment has to include the action element as well as changes in self-image. I refer the reader back to chapter 2 for a discussion of the literature.

Finally, it is, of course, crucial not to divorce the consideration of personal or collective empowerment from the context of an economic and political global system where even the nation state struggles to have any control over events.

7

Using the model: empowerment, gender, and development

*I like the term empowerment because no one has defined it clearly as yet; so it gives us a breathing space to work it out in action terms before we have to pin ourselves down to what it means. I will continue using it until I am sure it does **not** describe what we are doing.*[1]

At the beginning of this book I set myself the task of defining empowerment with a view to considering whether the concept has useful meaning in the gender and development debate and the practice arising from that debate. In this final chapter I shall draw out the implications of the model of empowerment that I outlined in the previous chapter and speculate on the way the model might be used in practice by individuals and organisations in working towards their own empowerment or that of others.

Empowerment as process

Empowerment, in the context of gender and development, is most usefully defined as a *process* (or processes) rather than an end product; it is dynamic and changing, and varies widely according to circumstance. I have focused in particular on empowerment which implies a definition of power that is generative and productive. The analysis of the case-study organisations shows that the empowerment process will take a form which arises out of a particular cultural, ethnic, historical, economic, geographic, political, and social location; out of an individual's place in the life cycle, specific life experience, and out of the interaction of all the above with gender relations prevailing in society. Despite such variety, there is a 'core' to the empowerment process common to different situations, which consists of increases in self-confidence and self-esteem, a sense of agency and of 'self' in a wider context, and a sense of *dignidad* (being worthy of and having a right to respect from others). If these core aspects of empowerment are encouraged and developed, women's self-perception will change and 'internalised oppression' will be challenged, contributing to increased 'power-to' and 'power from within'. The changes which result take many forms and may feed back into the process, with the individual better placed to make her own decisions and choices and better able to identify and act in her own interests. The extent to which the core qualities of empowerment for individuals or groups are developed depends on complex interactions between the factors which tend to encourage or inhibit the process.

An empowerment approach to development

When empowerment is defined more precisely, the notion of an empowerment approach to development for women becomes more useful as a tool for analysis and planning, whether in relation to personal empowerment, international relations, or intermediate contexts. It becomes possible to think more precisely about the process of empowerment; for example, a set of questions could be devised for a particular context to identify areas for action that would enhance the empowerment process. These questions fall into two groups, the first concerning an analysis of the 'core' elements of the process; the second relating to the encouraging and inhibiting elements of the situation:

- In what aspects of their lives is there self-confidence? Where is it lacking? Why?
- What are the elements of the situation which, through their presence or absence, encourage or inhibit self-confidence?
- Where do they have a sense of being able to act, to cause things to happen? Where do they not? Why? What kinds of decision-making do they actively participate in?
- How do they perceive themselves? In what ways do they limit themselves and their expectations?
- Do they have a sense of being worthy of the respect of others or them-selves?
- Do they relate to a wider context? What? Where is it limited? Why?

A second set of questions can then be formulated, related to planning and designing programmes, projects or activities:

- How could they tackle the issues identified by the earlier questions? What activities and methodologies are needed?

- What existing or new structures will be needed?

- What support or encouragement would make a difference? From whom?

- What might get in the way? How could that be minimised?

- What might encourage the process? How could that be strengthened?

- What changes might be expected?

- What methodology can be used that would be consistent with the empowerment process? How could it build on existing abilities and experience?

- What time-scale is appropriate?

- What are the internal power dynamics within the group?

- What are the power relationships between the group and a supporting organisation? What forms of power does the group have available to draw on?

Clearly, these questions can easily be made much more specific, and, by changing the 'they' to 'we' throughout, can be used for a participatory process of discussions and awareness-raising which itself has the potential to contribute to empowerment. In answering questions such as these, it is crucial to be aware of the danger that biases, prejudices, and preconceptions filter the responses, and therefore great care must be taken to question assumptions and probe beyond the easy or apparently self-evident answers. At the risk of stating the obvious, an empowerment approach requires thought and reflection, and great attention to its design. A deliberate empowerment approach is likely to raise issues which challenge established ways of doing things.

Empowerment as a gender issue

In the course of this discussion of empowerment and in examining the case studies, it has become clear that the empowerment of women is a *gender* issue and not simply a women's issue; it is also a class issue, a race issue, and so on, according to the various and changing identities people have. It is about transforming social relations. In tackling personal empowerment in its most basic form, the women in both the case studies had to confront gender conditioning and power relations in the decision to move outwards from the home into involvement in the group. Sometimes this literally meant obtaining their husband's permission to do so. For empowerment to happen within the women's close relationships with men, a re-negotiation of decision-making and resource-use patterns was needed, as well as a change of attitude on the part of the men. Empowerment of women is for women to experience; it does, however, require the behaviour of men to change, and this is perhaps illustrated most starkly in the re-negotiation of one-to-one intimate relationships. This was where women experienced the greatest difficulty, perhaps because each woman is here most bluntly confronted with her 'internalised oppression' (whereas in a group it is possible to 'ride with the tide' of empowerment of other group members); and because this is where she experiences 'power-over' in a very negative and immediate way (such as violence or lack of money). There is also the paradox, already mentioned, of these relationships being the site of support as well as disempowerment.

A woman may become personally empowered in many ways, including becoming able to earn her own living. However, if she continues to carry the full responsibility for domestic duties, including child-care, at the same time, her 'empowerment' has actually increased her burden. In some cases this also enables the man to take even less responsibility than before. A woman will often resolve the problem by devolving some of the work onto another woman and, commonly, onto her eldest daughter.

If empowerment of women is a gender issue, there is a need to tackle the corresponding task with men that will contribute to reducing the 'obstacle' of *machismo* (or its equivalent in other societies) and open up the possibilities of change in gender relations. This work has not had much recognition to date, and is very rare in the design of development programmes. There is, however, a growing realisation that attention needs to be paid to work with men on gender issues. In India, for example, gender trainers are increasingly working with mixed groups (Krishnamurthy, 1995), and there is a move to train men to be gender trainers, in order to overcome some of the difficulties women face in training men on gender issues. At a workshop on women's empowerment in Mexico in 1995, a major theme identified by women from grassroots organisations and from NGOs was the need to work with men to raise awareness and generate a commitment to change.

Work with men, as with women, on gender issues is multifaceted. Change needs to proceed in all the dimensions identified earlier in relation to empowerment processes. If men become less willing to use 'power over' in their relationships with women, whether in the home, in the workplace or in the community, it not only directly reduces the obstacles women face in their own empowerment process, but also helps to create an environment where the use of power in other forms becomes more possible.

Training alone cannot bring about the necessary changes. It is not sufficient, for example, to send field staff on a training course, if when they return they are unable to change the way they work because of policies or practices within the organisation which are incompatible with empowerment, and which are set by senior personnel who perhaps only pay lip-service to the need for change (and whose position might be under serious threat if such change were to materialise). Yet any organisation committed to the empowerment of women must address these challenges if it is to avoid developing a serious contradiction between its ideology and its practice. However, the empowerment of women, which is manifestly hampered by the unwillingness of men to relinquish 'power over', may also be the means by which positive change for men in their relationship to power will be achieved. Some women in PAEM, for example, described the way in which their increasing involvement, at their own insistence, in discussion with their partners about the use of family resources was leading the men to see that it was potentially beneficial to them to share responsibility for decision-making rather than carry it alone.

Empowerment as a development issue

The PAEM case study showed, with respect to the ambitious project of grain warehousing, that women who become empowered to act to meet their own needs can also contribute to development for the wider society. This differs from an 'efficiency approach' to women's development in that it is the women themselves who identify the need and the solution, rather than some external development agency or government body. There are many studies which show that women who receive education tend to have fewer children. Women with a lighter burden of domestic responsibilities are more able to take up opportunities for other activities. Empowered women, especially within an organisation where collective empowerment can become possible, are more likely to act to exert political pressure for change in favour of essential development needs. These may be economic needs, but may also be other kinds of development needs, such as the need for an effective state justice system through which women can invoke existing legal protections. In the Urraco case study there was an example of this, with some pressure being exerted by the Health Promotion team in the local community and nationally for the murderer of Nelly Suazo to be brought to justice.

How, then, might the concept of an empowerment approach to development be translated into practical action? I shall consider here three crucial, linked aspects: methodology, organisational structure, and the role of the 'change agent'. In addition, I shall address the issue of monitoring and evaluation as they relate to empowerment.

Methodological implications

If an empowerment approach is to be effective, it needs to foster the development of the core aspects of empowerment. It therefore requires a methodology that will in and of itself contribute to an increase in self-esteem, self-confidence, and so on, irrespective of the actual 'content' of activities. The methodology needs to be based on an attitude of complete respect for the women involved. The PAEM case illustrated this attitude clearly; there was an implicit assumption that the women had the capacity to achieve great things, and to take charge of their own empowerment processes. The methodology must in no way collude with the 'internalised oppression' that women carry. For example, a methodology that relies on some sort of 'promoter' to plan group activities, and does not actively involve women in the planning process, could reinforce an internalised belief that a women is not capable of planning or taking any kind of leadership. But an unquestioning acceptance of ideas put forward by women for activities, without challenging women's assumptions of what they are capable of or generating any understanding of how women's lives become limited, can also reinforce and collude with internalised oppression. This argument is important in debates about cultural imperialism. The right of any outsider to suggest a course of action that would change an existing cultural form has been strongly questioned, even where that form includes blatantly oppressive behaviours, on the grounds that it is an interference with cultural integrity. This argument has been frequently used against feminist opposition to such practices as female genital mutilation and dowry. An analysis of internalised oppression can explain the active role of women in maintaining and defending cultural traditions which perpetuate the subordination and mistreatment of women.

Women need to be free to act from their own analysis and priorities and not be manipulated by outsiders; yet the restrictions of internalised oppression, which limit women's options, must be challenged. If possible, a methodology should be adopted that will help women to perceive the limitations that they place on themselves. The booklet *Conociéndome a mí Misma* is part of such a methodology. It contrasts strongly with the Urraco teaching materials, which provide 'facts' to be learnt, with little process for understanding context, for self-analysis, or even for identifying subjects of importance.

The methodology should be flexible and creative: while there are activities and approaches which will be useful in many situations, a formulaic approach is unlikely to be successful. Attempts to replicate a successful outcome will always require fresh thinking. For the development organisation this can be a difficulty, partly because more human resources are likely to be required, and also because it becomes impossible to have a neat and tidy programme with uniform components which can be readily compared and reproduced. It also makes the process of monitoring and evaluating achievements much more demanding.

An analysis of the 'encouraging' elements and 'obstacles' facing the women will also have implications for methodology. In both the case studies, for example, the encouraging elements include 'travel'. If an analysis of the situation for women in a particular group or community implies that travel would contribute to empowerment, then a visit to meet women working on similar issues elsewhere in the country might be a useful activity to introduce. Similarly, the building of links with other organisations or communities and opportunities for networking can be valuable. Likewise with any 'obstacles': for example, if there is a culture of *caudillismo* (see chapter 3), the methodology could be designed expressly to minimise the possibility of reproducing that culture within the group, and ways of raising critical awareness about how *caudillismo* operates could be built into the programme content.

The significance of organisational structure

The two case studies illustrate the way in which organisational structure can influence the empowerment process. In Urraco, the programme design was based on a two-year course of study, and this structure limited the programme's capacity to encourage empowerment. The role that the co-ordinating team played in the functioning of the study circles also restricted empowerment, by fostering, however unintentionally, a sense of dependence. This is in sharp contrast to the PAEM structure, where animators were chosen by the groups from among their own members, so that various women filled the role at different times, and an open-ended programme gave scope for activities to develop in a very flexible way at the group's own pace. The *consejo* provided a forum where animators could find support, encouragement, and opportunities to think and learn about their leadership role and to plan and develop strategy. The zone meetings and annual assembly provided fora for women from the groups to meet each other, compare notes, travel out of their communities, and develop a sense of themselves as agents in a wider context.

Structural features can also serve to strengthen 'encouraging' aspects, such as leadership development, autonomy, and the identification of needs. In Urraco, there was some scope for developing leadership, in the circle co-ordinators. The structure, however, did not actively encourage the development of leadership skills by either circle co-ordinators or circle members, and there were very limited opportunities for new women to move into leadership roles. There was little scope for autonomy, as the programme was firmly associated with the Catholic church's Promoción Feminina. Also the programme came into being as a result of a need identified by outsiders. In contrast, the PAEM programme structure served to amplify the impact of many of the encouraging aspects, by building leadership development into the programme in an explicit way, by being set up with autonomy and self-management in mind from the outset, and by building the identification of needs, analysis, and understanding of the context directly into the materials and methodology.

Empowerment and the change agent

The role of the change agent in programmes intended to promote empowerment with women is potentially a pivotal one. Change agents are usually (though not always) outsiders; they are often extension workers, 'experts' in some form. The attitudes they bring to their work, and the form their work takes can have immense impact, positively or negatively, on the people with whom they work. With respect to empowerment, there are a number of attitudes and skills which are essential for a change agent to have, if women are to develop self-confidence, self-esteem, and a sense of themselves as able to act in a wider sphere. These attitudes include complete respect for each individual and for the group; humility and an eagerness for learning to be mutual; flexibility; and commitment to the empowerment process. The change agent should posses facilitation skills, active listening skills, and non-directive questioning skills.[2] Their role is essentially that of a catalyst — except that, unlike a chemical catalyst, the change agent is not likely to emerge unchanged at the end of the process.

All human beings are the product of their particular life-history and culture; it is vital for the change agent to have self-awareness in terms of their own biases, priorities and areas of similarity and difference in relation to the women they are working with. The training of change agents is an important issue. The skills and attitudes outlined above are not quickly acquired and require much practice and constant monitoring. How this might be achieved is the subject for another book and I shall not attempt to go into detail here. Training needs to be a continuous process, with opportunities for self-reflection and self-evaluation. As well as possessing the appropriate skill, a trainer needs to be perceived as legitimate if the training is to be effective, accepted, and implemented. In some cases this will mean that they need to be local rather than outsiders; in others, it may be the reverse! Much will depend on the cultural context, the acceptability of the ideas, whether these are seen as 'foreign', and whose interests the training is seen as supporting. Training may be formal, or may be an informal process. For example, in the PAEM case study, María Esther filled the role of change agent with the organisation; her training had been a mixture of some formal training and a lot of 'on-the-job' informal training, with constant analysis of the process, and appropriate support.

Implications for the supporting organisation

The role of organisations wishing to support processes of empowerment in grassroots groups or within local or national NGDOs is a major issue, about which much could be written. The constraints of space do not permit a full discussion here; all that can be done is to outline some of the problems and challenges.

The role of supporting organisations cannot, by definition, be a directing one. It is a role of solidarity, but not in a passive sense. The much-used term 'partnership' has some of the resonances needed, but it has become rather diluted through tokenistic use. I prefer to think in terms of building alliances.

Supporting organisations who see their role as allies to groups or organisations in the empowerment process may face problems in complying with the requirements of their own accountability processes. Reporting cycles, and criteria for success or failure as conditions for funding, provide pressures that work against an empowerment approach. For example, funding tied to short-term 'projects' brings pressure for quick, clearly visible, quantifiable results. Yet processes of empower-ment can take many years and may require an open-ended approach, with unpredictable and inconclusive outcomes. Within a 'project' perspective, not having reached certain objectives within a fixed length of time can be perceived as failure. Talk of 'empowerment projects' may indeed be a contradiction in terms, since the 'project' is generally seen as a short, (usually three to five years), specific cycle of activity with pre-determined objectives and targets. Adopting an empowerment approach involves women themselves setting the agenda and managing the pace of change.

Support for programmes designed to foster empowerment may present fund-raising dilemmas. The images that have encouraged charitable giving in the past have been the antithesis of empowerment images, or have been tangible images of, for example, new water systems or immunisation programmes. This implies the need for re-education of donors to respond to more positive, but less tangible images.

Supporting organisations may find it difficult to work alongside 'project partners' who have little interest in empowerment of women. Grassroots organisations, local and national NGDOs, and popular organisations, unless they are feminist women's organisations, are unlikely to have developed an empowerment approach. However, organisations looking for funds are quick to identify trends in funding criteria, and will strategically (or even cynically) include in funding applications currently 'fashionable' words, in order to obtain funding. 'Empowerment of women' has become one such phrase.

The complexity of women's lives and the inter-relatedness of the many issues that touch them can easily be lost sight of in the planning process. Any model of empowerment is a simplification of 'reality', but the model presented in this book is flexible and can be adapted to differing circumstances. The process of empowerment can be supported in many ways, some of which fall happily within other development approaches and many of which can be linked with tangible changes. A well can be built in a way that supports the empowerment of women, by encouraging them to do the necessary analysis and decision-making and to take control over their lives. Women can be taught to read in a way which generates debate and analysis and which supports them to become more confident and able to act. Any activities can be planned *with* people rather than *for* people. As Wieringa observes,

Any project concerned with women can potentially entail a transformative element. Sewing courses, literacy programmes, cooking lessons can be given in a way that allows for discussion of the gender division of labour, of women's control over their finances, of sexual violence.[3]

What the supporting organisation needs to look for is a leverage point. Taking an empowerment approach to work with women does, however, require the exploration of 'new' approaches, as well as a revision of the way in which 'old' approaches are used. For example, activities such as networking and the maintenance and strengthening of women's organisations take on a new significance within an empowerment approach. There may also be an appropriate lobbying role for the supporting organisation, though women can and will lobby on their own behalf.

The resources that supporting organisations bring to the empowerment process are not only financial. For example, in the PAEM case study, personal support at crucial moments was essential for the individual setting up the organisation; providing contacts with relevant individuals and organisations was also helpful.

The effectiveness with which a supporting organisation can foster empowerment processes for women will be adversely affected if its own organisational culture works against the empowerment of women. Issues of empowerment for women working for supporting organisations are extremely relevant to the development of an empowerment approach with 'partner' organisations, and there are important implications for management style and the involvement of women at all levels. Several women who work for development agencies as gender specialists have told me that their organisations systematically marginalise the work of the gender specialists while ostensibly having a commitment to women's empowerment.[4] If a separate women's or gender section exists within the organisation, there is a danger that this may have the effect of ghettoising the work.

There may be further contradictions between rhetoric and practice: for example, the organisation may use the language of partnership, but in practice keep a very tight control over what the 'partner' can do, requiring them to adhere to particular programme objectives even if circumstances change. There is a difficulty here: empowerment is not just about access to resources and opportunities, it is about *control* of those resources and opportunities. How can the supporting organisation relinquish control over resources, while maintaining its accountability and responsibility to donors? There is certainly no point in the organisation claiming to be anything other than what it is: integrity, honesty and transparency are essential in the organisation's dealings with its 'partners'. The incorporation of more flexibility into the supporting organisation's work will be necessary if an empowerment programme is to be effective by, for example, moving away from a project focus towards a more programmatic approach. In the case of PAEM, the women could develop their groups and activities without any particular outcomes being specified, but could still receive financial and other support from Oxfam. The supporting organisation had to take a risk: there was always a possibility that difficulties and conflicts, internally or externally, could have led to the collapse of the venture. If that had happened, it would not necessarily have meant that there had been no empowerment of the women involved; within a broader programme, this risk may be easier to take, especially if empowerment has been identified as a priority issue.

Evaluating empowerment

For development agencies to prioritise an empowerment approach and play an effective supporting role, it will be essential for them to be able to monitor and evaluate their work in an appropriate way. 'Performance indicators' of empowerment need to be developed, of which qualitative indicators will be most significant.[5] The methodology of the evaluation process is important, and women themselves must be actively involved in the negotiation of the criteria by which their empowerment will be evaluated; which could in itself enhance empowerment.[6]

What would constitute 'success' or 'progress' in terms of empowerment? With a detailed understanding of empowerment, within a particular context, it becomes possible to define the kinds of changes that might be expected to result from empowerment. Womankind Worldwide, a British NGO which has women's empowerment as an explicit aim, has established appraisal, monitoring and evaluation criteria, which include:

- the introduction of new ways of doing things — in child-care, in household, in livelihood, in local political arrangements;
- women refusing to continue old practices (eg genital mutilation, child marriage, taking daughters out of school, privileging sons etc.);
- women leaders at all levels;
- women advocating change within the community;
- women influencing other groups;
- women setting up their own self-help groups.

Because empowerment for each person or group is in a sense, a unique process, indicators must be flexible and wide-ranging, and are likely to change, possibly quite radically, over time. For a woman for whom it is a major challenge to attend meetings, initially her presence at meetings might be the measure of her empowerment; later, it might be her regular active contribution to discussion; later still, it might be her ability to initiate group activities. Given the often intangible and nebulous psychological and social processes involved, it can be easy, too, to miss the significance of particular events or inputs. Sometimes the impact of an activity will not be felt for quite some time. Yet conversely, it can be tempting to attribute a particular advance to a specific activity, with no evidence whether it would have happened anyway. Organisations should be humble about the work they do, and accept that it is not possible to define and measure every detail.

In conclusion

'Empowerment' is a word which may be used in imprecise and misleading ways in relation to women and processes of development, in part because of the contested nature of its underlying concept, power. The case studies presented here demonstrate that where 'empowerment' is used deliberately and there is clarity about the relevant kind of power concerned, it is a concept with the potential to be used creatively and effectively — both analytically and in practice — to facilitate women's development. This is particularly so if empowerment is seen as a process, within the changing and complex context of a gender-differentiated society, where women's life experiences may differ widely.

Any organisation working towards women's empowerment should use their own power deliberately and thoughtfully in ways which actively encourage empowerment, knowing that this process may take some time; that they cannot control the process; and that in some cases it may mean they themselves, as well as men within the society, having less of some forms of power. They must remain fully aware of, and be flexible enough to work with, the conflicts that may result from the changes in social relationships which empowerment brings about.

Endnotes

Preface

1 Much of the theory of non-violence grew out of the Gandhian model of passive resistance. It is concerned with how the apparently less powerful can draw on creative forms of resistance, often based on a strict moral code and on finding ways to make human contact with people in positions of power and authority. It can also be based on the power of nuisance value or of adverse publicity. The environmental campaigning work of Greenpeace is perhaps one of the best known and successful examples of nonviolent campaigning.

2 White, (1992) p. 22.

3 Kabeer, (1994) p. 91.

1 Introduction

1 World Bank (1989): _Sub-Saharan Africa: from crisis to sustainable growth,_ Washington D.C., World Bank. Quoted in Thomas (1992). My emphasis.

2 UNDP (1993) p. 21. My emphasis.

3 Various terms have been put forward to describe those countries where poverty is a current reality for a high proportion of the population. I have not yet found a term that is accurate as a collective noun for these countries and which avoids representing as an undifferentiated mass a group of countries which varies widely in size, resource base, population, character and so on. I use the term 'third world' in this book cautiously, as one which is generally understood even though it has become technically outdated with the demise of the 'Second World' of Socialist/ centrally planned countries, and to avoid for the most part more clumsy terms or expressions I like even less.

4 I do not intend here to give a complete account of the various theoretical developments, since they are well outlined elsewhere. I mention them here for historical and theoretical context rather than because they are essential to my argument. See, for example, Hunt (1989), Todaro (1994) and Toye (1987).

5 See, for example, Cornia, Jolly & Stewart (1987).

6 Todaro (1994)

7 See Schuurman (ed.) (1993) and Booth (1993).

8 See, for example, Nicholson (1990), Goetz (1991).

9 See Crush (1995), Escobar (1995).

10 See, for example, Egger (1986), Berger (1989), Rose (1992) and Kabeer (1994)

11 See, for example, Stöhr & Taylor (1981).

12 It is important to note that this has often been used in an instrumentalist way, using 'participation' to achieve other, often efficiency-related goals. See, for example, Shetty (1992) and Oakley et al. (1991).

13 I will not elaborate the arguments here, since they are well documented elsewhere. A particularly clear account can be found in Kabeer, (1994). See also Rathgeber (1990). WID theorists include Boserup (1970), Buvinic (1983), Tinker (1976) and Rogers (1980), to name just a few. Staudt (1985) gives an account of the history of WID in USAID.

14 Kabeer (1994 p.26.) quotes a World Bank position paper: 'If women continue to be left out of the mainstream of development and deprived of opportunities to realise their full potential, serious inefficiencies in the use of resources will persist.'

15 Jackson, (1994).

16 Rathgeber (1990).

17 Young (1988a) p. 6.

18 Kabeer, (1994).

19 Elson, (1991).

20 Moser (1989). A clear account of the 'Moser Gender Planning Framework', and of other approaches to gender planning, can be found in Williams (1995).

21 Molyneux, (1985).

22 Young, (1988b).

23 Alsop (1993) provides a clear critique of the practical/strategic framework in the context of gender planning in Northeast India, cautioning that the complexities of gender relations and social /economic factors and the limitations of 'projects' can easily lead to unintended outcomes, especially if 'outsiders' are identifying the needs/issues. She suggests that satisfying a practical need can positively support a strategic concern and that women need to be identifying the needs and issues for themselves.

24 Molyneux (1985); Moser (1989) and subsequently, many other writers.

25 Wieringa (1994) criticises the concept of practical/strategic gender needs or interests (and women's condition/position, on similar grounds) as theoretically flawed, since a) they change over time, b) they vary depending on who is defining them, c) they encourage a homogenisation of 'women's interests' where these are diverse, d) the distinction implies a hierarchical relation between the two which lends itself to a top-down approach, e) it is empirically impossible to distinguish between the two. She suggests that "the 'success' of certain development efforts may be better 'measured' by the way new interests surface or come to be defined along the way, than by the progress made in relation to certain interests which were defined during the planning stage". (p. 836).

26 In terms of quantity and quality. Most notably, from the women in the 'Development Alternatives with Women for a New Era' network, see Sen & Grown, (1988). Also Batliwala (1993).

27 See, for example, Batliwala (1993).

28 Chambers (1983) p. 214.

29 Ibid. p. 215.

30 Wasserstrom, (1985), p. 2. Emphasis in original.

31 See, for example, Yuval-Davies (1994)

Chapter 2

1   Dolan (1992)

2   See, for example, Bachrach and Baratz (1970), Lukes (1974), Foucault (1982), Giddens (1984), Hartsock (1985 and 1990), and Boulding (1988).

3   Lukes (1974)

4   See, for example, Hartsock (1985, 1990), and Starhawk (1987).

5 See, for example, Pheterson (1990), and Jackins (1983).

6 Nancy Hartsock (1985) draws on the writings of Hannah Arendt, Mary Parker Follett, Dorothy Emmett, Hannah Pitkin, and Berenice Carroll in her analysis.

7 Kelly (1992).

8 See Gordon (1980), Foucault (1982) ; Dreyfus & Rabinow (1982), Kritzman (1988).

9 Ibid, p. 242. Emphasis in original.

10 Foucault, in his later work, does show some awareness of this: "I don't believe that this question of 'who exercises power?' can be resolved unless that other question 'how does it happen?' is resolved at the same time" (1988b), p. 103. For me, however, this is not sufficient. Perhaps, had he lived longer, he would have provided a more satisfactory account!

11 Faith (1994). For an exploration of forms of resistance, see Scott (1985).

12 CCIC: *Two Halves make a Whole: Balancing Gender Relations in Development* quoted in Williams (1995), p. 234

13 ibid

14 I do not wish to imply here that there is one 'feminist' model of power. Space constraints have led me to generalise and leave out important variations in analysis.

15 McWhirter (1991).

16 Ward and Mullender (1991)

17 Parsons (1991).

18 Keller and Mbwewe (1991)

19 Moser (1989) p. 1815.

20 Price (n.d.) p. 6.

21 For example, Jesani (1990), Schenk-Sandbergen (1991), Kassam (1989), Watts (1991).

22 Friedmann (1992)

23 Freidmann does not present the household as an undifferentiated unit, and acknowledges power eimbalances within the household; nonetheless I find this a serious limitation on the usefulness of his account for considering the empowerment of women, in particular.

24 Thomas (1992)

25 Schumacher (1973)

26 Freire (1972). Freire does not use the term 'empowerment' in his early work. Interestingly, in his later work he specifically criticises any notion of empowerment as an individual phenomenon, or even as a community or social activity; rather, he insists on empowerment as 'social class empowerment': 'The question of social class empowerment involves how the working class, through its own experiences, its own construction of culture, engages itself in getting political power'. (Freire and Shore (1987) p. 112).

27 Johnson (1992) p.148

28 Ngau (1987)

29 Shetty (1992) p.8

30 After Molyneux, M (1981) *Women's Emancipation Under Socialism: A Model for the Third World* Brighton, IDS Publications.

31 Sen and Grown (1988)

32 Harold (1991) spells out in detail the workshop methodology on which her model is based and from the use of which the content of the CariWheel was developed. As well as the creation of categories and clusters, the workshop included a process of self-grading in relation to the categories the group chose as most significant, on a scale of 1-5, producing a polygonal 'map' of its self-perception.

33 For example, see Lean (1996): *Bread, Bricks and Belief: Communities in Charge of their Future.* Kumarian Press. Also, in October 1996, the World Bank held its first conference on the links in spiritual values and sustainable development.

34 Kabeer (1994b)

35 Dighe & Jain (1989) `Women's Development Programme: Some Insights into Participatory Evaluation', *Prashasnika* Vol. 18 Nos. 1-4 pp77-98 quoted in Kabeer (1993) p. 262.

36 Batliwala (1993) and (1994).

37 Yuval-Davis (1994).

38 Young (1993)

39 For example, this is presumably reflected in the inclusion of the term in Oxfam's Gender and Development Policy adopted in 1993: "[Oxfam] is committed to... developing positive action to promote the full participation and empowerment of women in existing and future programmes so as to ensure that Oxfam's programme benefits men and women equally". Oxfam (1993) p. 4.

Chapter 3

1 World Bank (1994).

2 Lapper and Painter (1985).

3 Barry and Norsworthy (1990).

4 EIU (1994).

5 'Our political objectives for Honduras are clear: to strengthen democracy and democratic institutions, to elicit full cooperation against nondemocratic forces in the region, to encourage regional cooperation and solidarity, and to obtain the greatest Honduran support possible for our objectives in the region and elsewhere. Our economic objectives must bolster and reinforce our overall objectives which can and would be undermined if political and social progress is not achieved.' Assistant Secretary of State, Elliot Abrams, quoted in Barry and Norsworthy (1990), p.111.

6 EIU (1994).

7 EIU Country Profile, 1994–5.

8 Barry and Norsworthy (1990).

9 Dunkerley (1988).

10 Latin American societies are heaviily dominated by social structures of kinship and patron-client relations. The latter involves complex sets of mutual obligation, for example, a landlord will help a tenant in hard times in exchange for the tenant's vote at election time. For a concise description of Latin American social relations, see Cubitt (1988).

11 Dunkerley (1988).

12 Barry and Norsworthy (1990).

13 World Bank (1994).

14 Central Bank/CEPAL figures quoted in CEM (1992).

15 CEM (1992).

16 Kawas & Zúñiga (1991).

17 *Tiempo*, 11.5.93.

18 World Bank (1994).

19 Benjamin (1987).

20 Caballero Zeitun (1988).

21 From 57 to 46 deaths per 1,000 live births: USAID figures.

22 In her work on Western Europe and North America, Walby concludes that "...patriarchy is composed of six structures: the patriarchal mode of production, patriarchal relations in paid work, patriarchal relations in the state, male violence, patriarchal relations in sexuality, and patriarchal relations in cultural institutions." This does not necessarily provide an accurate definition for Latin America but offers a useful guide. (Walby, 1990 p20).

23 See, for example, Caballero (1988); CEM, Centro de Estudios de la Mujer (1992).

24 Acker (1988).

25 World Bank (1994). There is no definition of 'married' given. Neither does the World Bank figure indicate whether or not sterilization is included in the definition of contraceptive methods.

26 CEM, (1992). There is no indication of the year for which this applies, thought they state their general sources as the 1988 census and the 1989 Household Survey.

27 Secretaria Ejecutiva del Gabinete Social (1992).

28 CEM (1992).

29 The economically active population is defined in the census as people aged ten or over who are engaged in economic activity, ie. in an occupation that brings them money, working for someone else, whether paid or not, and including people looking for work. There is no indication of whether or not this included women who 'help' on the family plot, although it is likely that it does not.

30 Howard-Borjas, (1989).

31 Kawas & Zúñiga (1991). However, Kuhn (1990) refers to a USAID document which puts forward that women's unpaid agricultural activity is much greater than might be suggested by official figures: of rural women, 59 per cent participate in sowing, 41 per cent in digging/hoeing, 39 per cent in harvesting and 22 per cent in weeding. Buvinic (n.d.) makes a strong case for disbelief of census data on women's agricultural activity, citing seasonal factors/timing of census interviews and the fact that for many women economic activity is not the 'primary activity' that census questions relate to. She also points out the fact that women she interviewed continued to perceive themselves as housewives even if they undertake income-generating activities.

32 Secretaria Ejecutivo del Gabinete Social, (1992).

33 Kuhn (1990).

34 Survey referred to in Howard-Borjas (1989).

35 The head of household is defined as the person who is recognised as such by other household members and who exercises authority through the making of decisions which affect the family group.

36 Secretaria Ejecutivo del Gabinete Social, (1992).

37 Mendoza (1988).

38 Central America Report, Spring 1989.

39 This account is based on Hilhorst, 1989 p. 13-15 and Kuhn, 1990 p134–6.

40 CEDOH Bulletin No. 159, July 1994

41 I use the term NGDO rather than the more common NGO, to emphasise the point that not all non-government organisations have a development focus or intent. The all-inclusive term NGO can include, for example, sports associations.

42 Kuhn (1990).

43 USAID (1982). A member of AID staff in Honduras who asked not to be identified commented to me that the rhetoric is in place but the practice is not.

Chapter 4

1 CNTC (1988).

2 Thanks to Andrés Albarenge Martinez of the Urraco Literacy Programme for information on literacy in the area.

3 *Tiempo* 25/8/92.

4 Urraco Pueblo group.

5 Andres Albarengue Martinez.

6 Werner (1989).

7 There is a debate about the value of child weighing programmes; they can be seen as experts telling the mother what she already knows.

8 The Concern Progresso office had funding from Oxfam UK/I for two years (Deborah Eade, personal communication).

9 I have a photograph of Marcela lying in a hammock outside a *champita*, a roughly built hut, in the middle of a banana plantation, totally engrosed in a copy of *mujer/fempress*, the Chilean feminist magazine!

Chapter 5

1 Tábora (1992).

2 See, for example, Posner and McPherson (1982).

3 The contribution of women to agricultural production varies widely throughout Latin America (see, for example, Deere and León, (1987)). It also varies through Honduras. See also Townsend (1993) on processes of 'housewifeization' on the agricultural frontier.

4 Respectability is an important issue. See Townsend (1995).

5 'Animator' is a term used to describe someone whose role is to motivate individuals to participate in group activities and to motivate the group to continue to meet and be active.

6 Tábora (1992) p96

7 Occupation of private land, known by some as 'land invasion'. The occupation of unproductive land was in certain circumstances permitted under the Agrarian Reform law of 1976.

8 María Esther Ruiz uses such words as *formación*, training, transformation and autonomy; she 'would steer clear of any word or phrase with power in it, such as *aceso a poder* (access to power) ... It suggests to me that María Esther and others are clearer than outside commentators that empowerment derives from the root word power, and that this is something about which to exercise caution in how you describe your intentions, especially in a culture which imagines that feminism is only about wresting power from men, rather than challenging the basis of power.' (Deborah Eade, personal communication.)

9 Indeed, there was a 'terror of feminism' (Deborah Eade, personal communication), with feminism seen as a Western, man-hating diversion that would weaken the popular movement. This has been a common view of feminism in many Third World countries, where a particular version of Western feminism has been equated with feminism. The growth of local feminist movements in Latin America has shown that, far from being a Western, elitist, imported indulgence, feminism is highly relevant and takes its own form in each location. See Vargas (1990&1991) and Mohanty (1991).

10 See, for example,Jackins (1983).

11 This is part of a wider debate amongst Latin American feminists in the popular movement. For some, the concept of autonomy is similar to at least part of the concept of empowerment as presented here. See, for example, Meynen & Vargas (1994) and Meertens (1994).

Chapter 6

1 There is, of course, a vast literature on the development of the self. Fogel (1993) contends that the human mind and sense of self must be seen as developing out of the processes of communication and relationship formation (in which culture is a central part) between the subject and other individuals.

2 For many women this distinction between her own needs and the needs of others did not appear to have meaning: my question about her own needs was almost always answered with reference to the needs of others. In other words, the meeting of others' needs was perceived as her *own* need. It was the more visible leaders who were able to distinguish between the two. This illustrates the cultural embeddedness of 'woman-as-carer', especially in relation to 'practical gender needs'.

3 See Eade & Williams (1995), Chapter on Financing Health Care.

Chapter 7

1 Unidentified NGO activist quoted in Batliwala (1993) p. 49. Emphasis in original.

2 It did not surprise me, for example, to find a section on 'listening skills' in the Oxfam Gender Training Manual (Williams, 1995).

3 Wieringa (1994) p. 843.

4 Personal communications; the individual concerned did not wish to be identified.

5 See, for example, Feuerstein (1986).

6 Womankind (1994, internal draft document).

Glossary of Spanish words used in the text

aldeas small village
ambiente environment
animadora animator
aplastada flattened, crushed (referring to female)

bajareque 'wattle and daub'
barrio(s) neighbourhood(s), slum(s)
botiquín first aid post, medicine chest

cacique political boss/'strong man' (local level)
caciquismo style of leadership/culture based on rule by (local) political bosses
campesino/a peasant
caseríos hamlet, settlement
caseta hut, small building
caudillo political boss/'strong man' (national level)
caudillismo style of leadership/culture based on rule by (national) political bosses
celebración de la palabra church service taken by a lay preacher
centavos cents
champita roughly built hut, hovel
clausura closing ceremony, graduation
clubes de amas de casa housewives clubs
compañero comrade/partner
consejo council

delegados delegates
delegado de la palabra delegate of the word: lay preacher

dignidad literally, dignity. In Spanish this has the meaning of self-esteem and worth, with an expectation of being seen by others as having worth and value

dinámicas dynamics — exercises

directiva management committee

empacadora packing plant

encuentro meeting

encuentro de zona zone meeting

enlace network

fincas farm

grupos campesinos peasant groups/co-operatives

guaro maize liquor

hechería witchcraft

latifundista owner of a large estate

lempira Lempira — Honduran unit of currency

leña firewood

machismo male pride, male chauvinism

machista full of *machismo*

manzana land measure: 1.75 acres

maquila assembly plant; factory in export processing zone

milpa maize plot

minifundios small farm

mujer woman

municipio municipality

padre father

pareja partner, couple

patronato village council

parcelero farmer working small farm

pecadosin

pena grief, sorrow, regret

plan básico basic secondary curriculum

platanera banana plantation

prestaciónes range of benefits and payment made on leaving a job

problematica set of problems, issues

Promoción Femenina the Catholic church's organisation for pastoral work with women

punta Garífuna dance

quehaceres household chores

sectorial(es) sectoral meeting(s)

sociodrama role-play

tamalesa maize food
tortilla flat maize bread, the staple food

unión libre common-law marriage

vicios vices — alcohol, sex, drugs.

Bibliography

Acker, A (1988) *Honduras: The Making of a Banana Republic*, Toronto, Between the lines.

Adams, R (1990) *Self-Help, Social Work and Empowerment*, Basingstoke, Macmillan.

Albrecht, L and Brewer, R M (eds.) (1990) *Bridges of Power: Women's Multicultural Alliances*, Philadelphia, New Society Publishers.

Alsop, R (1993) 'Whose Interests? Problems in Planning for Women's Practical Needs', *World Development* 21: 3, pp367–377.

Anderson, M B and Woodrow, P J (1989) *Rising from the Ashes: Development Strategies in Times of Disaster* , Boulder Westview Press.

Anderson, T P (1988a) 'Politics and the Military in Honduras' in *Current History* December, pp. 425–431.

_____ (1988b) *Politics in Central America: Guatemala, El Salvador, Honduras and Nicaragua*, New York, Praeger.

Antrobus, P (1989) 'The Empowerment of Women' in Gallin, R S, Aronoff, M and Ferguson A (1989) *The Women and International Development Annual, Vol. 1*, Boulder, Westview Press, pp. 189–208.

Ara, A and Marchand, B (1993) *Buscando Remedio Escuela de Salud Pública de Nicaragua*, Centro de Investigaciones y Estudios de la Salud (CIES) and Universidad Autonoma de Nicaragua. Managua, Nicaragua (Revised Edition).

Arac, J (ed.) (1988) *After Foucault: Humanistic Knowledge, Postmodern Challenges*, New Brunswick, Rutgers University Press.

Araki, M (1991) 'Towards Empowerment of Women in the Third World: The Training of the Change Agent' Unpublished MA thesis, Reading University.

Archer, D and Costello, P (1990) *Literacy and Power: the Latin American Battleground*, London, Earthscan.

Bachrach, P and Baratz, M S (1970) *Power and Poverty: Theory and Practice,* New York, Oxford University Press.

Barnes, B (1988) *The Nature of Power,* Cambridge, Polity Press.

Barnet, E H (1981) 'The Development of Personal Power for Women: an Exploration of the Process of Empowerment' Unpublished Ed. D. Dissertation, Boston University School of Education.

Barry, T and Norsworthy, K (1990) *Honduras: A Country Guide,* Albuquerque, New Mexico, Inter-Hemispheric Education Resource Center .

Batliwala, S (1993) *Empowerment of Women in South Asia: Concepts and Practices,* New Delhi, FAO-FFHC/AD.

Benjamin, M (ed.) (1987) *Don't be Afraid Gringo: A Honduran Woman Speaks from the Heart — The Story of Elvia Alvarado,* San Francisco, Institute of Food and Development Policy.

Bennett, R J, Wicks, P and McCoughan, A (1994) *Local Empowerment and Business Services: Britain's experiment with Traning and Enterprise Councils,* London, UCL Press.

Berger, M (1989) 'Giving Women Credit: The Strengths and Limitations of Credit as a Tool for Alleviating Poverty' in *World Development* 17:7, pp. 1017-1032.

Berninghausen, J and Kerstan, B (1992) *Forging New Paths: Feminist Social Methodology and Rural Women in Java,* London, Zed Books.

Bhasin, K (1985) *Towards Empowerment,* New Delhi, FAO-FFHC/AD.

Blanco, G and Valverde, J (1990) *Honduras: Iglesia y Cambio Social* Tegucigalpa, Editorial Guaymuras.

Bock, G and James, S (eds.) (1992) *Beyond Equality and Difference: Citizenship, Feminist Politics and Female Subjectivity,* London, Routledge.

Bookman, A and Morgen, S (eds.) (1988) *Women and the Politics of Empowerment,* Philadelphia, Temple University Press.

Booth, D (1985) 'Marxism and Development Sociology: Interpreting the Impasse'in *World Development* 13: 7.

_____ (1993) 'Development Research: from Impasse to a new Agenda' in Schuurman, F (ed.) (1993), pp. 49–76.

_____ (ed.)(1994) *Rethinking Social Development: Theory, Research and Practice,* London, Longman.

Boserup, E (1970) *Women's Role in Economic Development,* New York, St. Martin's Press.

Boulding, K (1988) *Three Faces of Power,* London, Sage.

Brockett, C D (1987a) 'Public Policy, Peasants and Rural Development in Honduras' in *Journal of Latin American Studies* 19, pp. 69–86.

_____ (1987b) 'The Commercialisation of Agriculture and Rural Economic Insecurity: The case of Honduras' in *Studies in Comparative International Development* Spring 1987 pp. 82–102.

Brunt, D (1992) *Mastering the Struggle: Gender Actors and Agrarian Change in a Mexican Ejido,* Latin American Studies No. 64, Amsterdam, CEDLA.

Bryman, A (1988) *Quantity and Quality in Social Research,* London, Unwin Hyman.

Bujra, J (1993) 'Gender, Class and Empowerment: A Tale of Two Tanzanian Servants' in *Review of African Political Economy* 56, pp. 68–78.

Burgess, R G (1984) *In the Field: An Introduction to Field Research,* London, Unwin Hyman.

_____ (ed.)(1992) *Studies in Qualitative Methodology Vol. 3: Learning about Fieldwork,* Greenwich, Conn. Jai Press Inc.

Buvinic, M (1983) 'Women's Issues in Third World Poverty: a Policy Analysis' in *Women and Poverty in the Third World* (ed) Buvinic, M, Lycette, M and McGreevey, W P, Baltimore, Johns Hopkins University Press, pp 14–33.

_____ (n.d.) 'La Productora Invisible en el Agro Centroamericano: Un Estudio de Caso en Honduras' in Leon, M. (ed.) *Las Trabajadoras del Agro Asociación Columbiana para el Estudio de la Población,* Bogotá, Colombia, pp. 103–111.

Caballero Zeitun, E L (1988) *La Situación de la Mujer en Honduras,* Tegucigalpa, Uno+Uno Consultores.

_____ (1989) *La Contribución Economica de la Mujer en la Construcción de la Sociedad,* Tegucigalpa, UNICEF/ CEPROD/ CCD/EDUCSA.

_____ *et al* (1992a) *Sondeo Sobre las Condiciónes de Trabajo y Contratación de las Mujeres que Laboren en la Maquila,* Tegucigalpa, Uno+Uno Consultores.

_____ *et al* (1992b) *Las que Trabajan Más para Ganar Menos: Las Mujeres Urbanas y la Crisis en los 90s,* Tegucigalpa, Uno+Uno Consultores/Fundación Friedrich Ebert.

Caballero Zeitun, E L and Sánchez Lam, C L (1991) *Las Manos Indispensables: La Mujer Pobre Como Protagonista de la Acción Social,* Tegucigalpa, Uno+Uno Consultores.

Caballero Zeitun, E L, Ramos Suazo, M E and Sánchez Lam, C L (1992) *Derechos Humanos y Reproductivos: Una Aproximación a la Problemática de la Mujer Hondureña,* Tegucigalpa, Uno+Uno Consultores.

Cambio Empresarial 5/12, 1992 'La Mujer Hondureña en Cifras'

Canadian Council for International Co-operation (1991) 'Two Halves Make a Whole: Balancing Gender Relations in Development' Ottawa, mimeo.

Carpeta Popular 1/12.1992 'Una Aproximación a la Cultura Nacional'.

_____ 1/27, 1993 'La Mujer en Honduras'.

_____ 1/33, 1993 'El Trabajo Visible de la Mujer Hondureña'.

CEDOH (1989) *La Conexión USA: Directorio de las Organisaciones No Gubernamentales en Honduras con Vínculos an los Estados Unidos,* Tegucigalpa, CEDOH. *Central America Report* (Spring 1989).

Centro de Documentación de Honduras (1994) *Boletín Informativo* No. 159. Tegucigalpa, CEDOH.

Centro de Estudios de la Mujer (1992) *Actualización de Diagnostico Sobre la Situación de la Mujer en Honduras,* Tegucigalpa, CEM.

CEPAL (1994) *Statistical Yearbook for Latin America and the Caribbean,* Santiago, Chile, United Nations.

Chambers, R (1983) *Rural Development: Putting the Last First,* London, Longman.

_____ (1994) 'All Power Deceives' *IDS Bulletin* 25: 2, April.

Chambers, R, Pacey, A and Thrupp, L A (1989) *Farmer First: Farmer Innovation and Agricultural Research,* London, Intermediate Technology Publications.

Checkoway, B and Norsman, A (1986) 'Empowering Citizens with Disabilities' in *Community Development Journal* 21:4.

del Cid, R, Noé Pino, H and Hernández, A (1982) *Honduras: Crisis Económica y Proceso de Democratisación Politica,* Tegucigalpa, CEDOH.

Clegg, S R (1989) *Frameworks of Power,* London, Sage.

CNTC (1988) *Nuestra Realidad Campesina,* Tegucigalpa, Editorial Guaymuras.

Cockerill, S (1992) 'Equality and Empowerment: The Principles of the Youth Work Curriculum?' in *Youth and Policy* 36, March 1992, pp. 17–21.

COIPRODEN (1993) *Las Niñas y los Niños: El Presente de Honduras,* Tegucigalpa, COIPRODEN.

Collins, P H (1990) *Black Feminist Thought: Knowledge, Consciousness and the Politics of Empowerment,* London, Routledge.

Comisión de la Mujer (1991) *Informe de Labores de la Comisión de la Mujer, Periodo Marzo-Octubre 1991,* Tegucigalpa, Congreso Nacional.

Comité para la Defensa de los Derechos Humanos en Honduras (1992) *Situación de los Derechos de a Mujer en Honduras,* Tegucigalpa, CODEH.

Constantino-David, K (1982) 'Issues in Community Organization' in *Community Development Journal* 17:3.

Cornia, G A, Jolly, R and Stewart, F (eds.) (1987) *Adjustment with a Human Face, Vol. 1: Protecting the Vulnerable and Promoting Growth,* Oxford, Clarendon Press.

Cotterill, P (1992) 'Interviewing Women: Issues of Friendship, Vulnerability and Power' in *Women's Studies International Forum* 15/5-6, pp. 593–606.

Craig, G, Mayo, M and Taylor, M (1990) 'Editorial Introduction. Empowerment: A Continuing Role for Community Development' in *Community Development Journal* 25:4, pp. 286–290.

Crowley, H and Himmelweit, S (1992) *Knowing Women: Feminism and Knowledge*, Cambridge, Polity Press with the Open University.

Crush, J (1995) *Power of Development*, London, Routledge.

Cubitt, T (1988) *Latin American Society*, Harlow, Longman.

Currer, C (1992) 'Strangers or Sisters? An Exploration of Familiarity, Strangeness and Power in Research' in Burgess, R G (ed.)(1992) pp. 1–32.

Dahl, R A (1961) *Who Governs? Democracy and Power in an American City*, New Haven and London: Yale University Press.

Davis, A (1988) 'Radical Perspectives on the Empowerment of Afro-American Women: Lessons for the 1980s' in *Harvard Educational Review* 58:3, pp. 348–353.

Davis, K, Leijenaar, M, Oldersma, J (eds) (1991) *The Gender of Power*, London, Sage.

Deere, C D (1985): 'Rural Women and State Policy: The Latin American Agrarian Reform Experience' in *World Development* 13:9, pp. 1037–1053.

Deere, C D and León, M (1987) *Rural Women and State Policy: Feminist Perspectives on Latin American Agricultural Development*, Boulder, Westview Press.

Devaux, M (1994) 'Feminism and Empowerment: A Critical Reading of Foucault' in *Feminist Studies* 20:2 pp. 223–247.

Diamond, I and Quinby, L (eds.)(1988) *Feminism and Foucault: Reflections on Resistance*, Boston, Northeastern University Press.

Días, E, Caballero, E L, Canales, B H and Cáceres, M (1992) *Balance de las Acciones de Compensación Social en Relación al Plan de Acción Nacional*, Tegucigalpa, PNUD/UNICEF.

Díez, Z, del Amo, I, Aguiluz, E and Gil, H (1991) *25 Años de Presencia Pasionista en Honduras, C.A. (1965-1990)*, Santa Bárbara, Honduras, Vicaría Episcopal de Santa Bárbara.

Dolan, C (1992) 'British Development NGOs and Advocacy in the 1990s' in Edwards and Hulme (1992) pp. 203–210.

Dreyfus, H L and Rabinow, P (1982) *Michel Foucault: Beyond Structuralism and Hermaneutics*, Brighton, Harvester Press.

Duelli Klein, R (1983) 'How to do what we want to' in Bowles, G and Duelli Klein, R (eds.) (1983) *Theories of Women's Studies*, London, Routledge pp. 88–104.

Dunkerley, J (1988) *Power in the Isthmus*, London, Verso Press.

Eade, D (1991) '"If I don't know who I am...": Women's Awareness Training in Honduras, Central America' in *GADU Pack No 14* Oxford, Oxfam.

Eade, D and Williams, S (1995) *Oxfam Handbook of Development and Relief*, Oxford, Oxfam.

Economist Intelligence Unit (1994) *Country Profile, 1994-95: Honduras, Nicaragua*, London, The Economist.

Edwards, M (1989) 'The Irrelevance of Development Studies' in *Third World Quarterly* 11: 1, pp 116–136.

Edwards, M (1993) 'How Relevant is Development Studies' in Schuurman F (ed.) (1993).

Edwards, M and Hulme, D (eds.) (1992) *Making a Difference: NGOs and Development in a Changing World*, London, Earthscan.

Edwards, R (1990) 'Connecting Method and Epistemology: A White Woman Interviewing Black Women' in *Women's Studies International Forum* 13:5, pp. 477–490.

Egger, P (1986) 'Banking for the Rural Poor: Lessons from some Innovative Savings and Credit Schemes' in *International Labour Review* 125:4, pp. 447–462.

El Heraldo, Tegucigalpa

Elshtain, J B (1992) 'The Power and Powerlessness of Women' in Bock, G and James, S (eds.) (1992), pp. 110–125.

Elson, D (ed.) (1991) *Male Bias in the Development Process*, Manchester, Manchester University Press.

ESA Consultores (1993) *Update of Baseline Study of Honduras Export Processing Zones*, Tegucigalpa, Price Waterhouse/USAID.

Escobar, A (1995) *Encountering Development: The Making and Remaking of the Third World*, Princeton, Princeton University Press.

Everett, J (1989) 'Incorporation versus Conflict: Lower Class Women, Collective Action and the State in India' in Charlton, S E, Everett, J and Staudt, K (eds) (1989) *Women, the State and Development*, New York, State University of New York Press. pp. 152–176.

Faith, K (1994) 'Resistance: Lessons from Foucault and Feminism' in Radtke and Stam (1994), pp.36–66.

Feuerstein, M (1986) *Partners in Evaluation*, London, Macmillan.

Financial Times 'Honduras Legislates for Farm Recovery', by Ian Walker, 20.3.1992, p.30

FLACSO (1991) *Inventario de Organisaciones que Trabajan con la Mujer en Centroamérica*, San José, Costa Rica, Fundación Arias.

Flax, J (1992) 'Beyond Equality: Gender, Justice and Difference' in Bock, G and James, S (eds.) (1992).

Fogel, A (1993) *Developing through Relationships: Origins of Communication, Self and Culture*, Chicago, University of Chicago Press.

Folbre, N (1994) *Who pays for the kids? Gender and the Structures of Constraint*, London, Routledge.

Fonow, M M and Cook, J A (eds.) (1991) *Beyond Methodology: Feminist Scholarship as Lived Research*, Bloomington, Indiana University Press.

Foucault, M (1982) 'The Subject and Power', Afterword in Dreyfus and Rabinow (1982).

_____ (1988a) *Politics, Philosophy, Culture: Interviews and other writings 1977-1984* ed. L D Kritzman, New York, Routledge.

_____ (1988b) 'Truth, Power, Self: an interview with Michel Foucault' in Martin, L, Gutman, H and Hutton, P (eds.) (1988) *Technologies of the Self: a Seminar with Michel Foucault*, London, Tavistock.

Fowler, A (1991a)'The Role of NGOs in changing state-Society Relations: Perspectives from Eastern and Southern Africa', *Development Policy Review* 9:1, pp. 53–84, Overseas Development Institute, Sage.

Fowler, A (1991b) 'Building Partnerships between Northern and Southern development NGOs: issues for the 1990s' in *Development in Practice* 1:1, pp. 5–18.

_____ (1992) 'Non-Governmental Organisations as Agents of Democratization: An African Perspective'. Paper given to the Development Studies Association NGO Study Group. London, March.

Francis, E (1993) 'Qualitative Research: Collecting Life Histories' in Devereux, S and Hoddinott, J (eds.)(1993) *Fieldwork in Developing Countries*, Boulder, Lynne Reinner Publishers.

Fraser, N (1989) *Unruly Practices: Power, Discourse and Gender in Contemporary Social Theory*, Cambridge, Polity Press.

Freire, P (1972) *Pedagogy of the Oppressed*, Harmondsworth, Penguin Books.

_____ (1973) *Education: the Practice of Freedom*, London, Writers and Readers Publishing Co-operative.

Freire, P and Shore, I (1987) *A Pedagogy for Liberation: Dialogues on Transforming Education*, Basingstoke, Macmillan.

Friedmann, J (1992) *Empowerment: The Politics of Alternative Development*, Oxford, Blackwell.

Funes, M A (1991a) 'Crisis en la Década del 80 y Reestructuración de la Economia' *Boletín Especial No. 53*, Tegucigalpa, CEDOH.

Funes, M A (1991b) 'El Desafio del Movimiento Popular para la Decada de los Años 90' in *Boletín Especial No. 54*, Tegucigalpa, CEDOH.

Giddens, A (1977) *New Rules of Sociological Method*, London, Hutchinson

_____ (1984) *The Constitution of Society*, Cambridge, Polity Press.

Gilbert, A (1994) *The Latin American City*, London, Latin America Bureau.

Glaser, B G and Strauss, A L (1967) *The Discovery of Grounded Theory: Strategies for Qualitative Research*, New York, Aldine de Gruyter.

Glover, D J (1986) 'Agrarian Reform and Agro-Industry in Honduras' in *Canadian Journal of Development Studies* 7:1, pp. 21–35.

Goetz, A M (1991) 'Feminism and the Claim to Know: Contradictions in Feminist Approaches to Women in Development' in Grant, R and Newland, K (eds.) *Gender and International Relations*, Milton Keynes, Open University Press.

_____ (1994) 'From Feminist Knowledge to Data for Development: The Bureaucratic Management of Information on Women and Development' in *IDS Bulletin* 25:2, pp. 27–36.

Gómez, R (1993) 'La Participación de la Mujer Hondureña en el Desarollo del Pais: Principales Desafíos' Tegucigalpa, mimeo.

Gordon, C (ed.) (1980) *Power/Knowledge: Selected Interviews and Other Writings*, Brighton, Harvester Press.

Gruber, J and Trickett, E J (1987) 'Can we Empower Others? The Paradox of Empowerment in the Governing of an Alternative Public School' in *American Journal of Community Psychology* 15:3, pp. 353–371.

Guba, E (ed.)(1990a) *The Paradigm Dialog*, Newbury Park, Ca. Sage.

_____ (1990b) 'The Alternative Paradigm Dialog' in Guba, E (1990a), pp.17–30.

Gutierrez, L M (1990a) 'Ethnic Consciousness, Consciousness Raising and the Empowerment Process in Latinos'. Unpublished PhD thesis, Ann Arbor, University of Michigan.

_____ (1990b) 'Working with Women of Colour: an Empowerment Perspective' in *Social Work*, March 1990.

Gutierrez, L M and Ortega, R (1991)'Developing Methods to Empower Latinos: the Importance of groups' *Social Work with Groups* 14:2, 23–43.

Hall, C M (1992) *Women and Empowerment: Strategies for Increasing Autonomy*, Washington, Hemisphere Publishing Corporation.

Hammersley, M (1992) *What's Wrong with Ethnography?*, London, Routledge.

Hammersley, M and Atkinson, P (1983) *Ethnography: Principles in Practice*, London, Routledge.

Haraway, D (1985) 'A Manifesto for Cyborgs: Sciences, Technology and Socialist Feminism in the 1980s' in *Socialist Review* 80, pp. 65–107.

_____ (1988) 'Situated Knowledges: The Science Question in Feminism and the Privelege of Partial Perspective' in *Feminist Studies* 14:3.

Harding, S (1991) *Whose Science? Whose Knowledge? Thinking from Women's Lives*, Milton Keynes, Open University Press.

Harold, J (1991) 'Empowerment: A Feminist Approach to Understanding and Action', Unpublished M.Sc. thesis, University of Guelph.

_____ (1994a) 'Death, Life and Empowerment in West Indian Women's Groups' in *Women and Environment*, Summer/Fall 1994 pp. 16–17.

_____ (1994b) 'Are We Empowered Yet? A Workshop for Groups' in *Women and Environment*, Summer/Fall 1994, pp. 18–20.

Hartsock, N (1985) *Money, Sex and Power: Towards a Feminist Historical Materialism*, Boston, Northeastern University Press.

_____ (1990) 'Foucault on Power: a Theory for Women?' in Nicholson, L J (ed) *Feminism/Postmodernism*, New York and London, Routledge, 157–175.

Harvey, D (1985) in *Professional Geographer* 1:1.

Hernandez Chávez, A (1984) 'Política Económica y Pensamiento Neoliberal: El Caso de Honduras' in *Estudios Sociales Controamericanos* 37, pp. 231-257.

Hernandez, T and Murguialday, C (1991) *Mujeres, Desarrollo y Políticas de Cooperación: Aportes para la Discusión desde una Perspectiva de Género*, Nicaragua, Puentos de Encuentro.

Hilhorst, T (1989) *La Situación de la Mujer Campesina y sus Formas de Organisación*, Tegucigalpa, SNV.

Hooks, B (1984) *Feminist Theory: From Margin to Center*, Boston, Southend Press.

_____ (1990) *Yearning: Race, Gender and Cultural Politics*, Boston, South End Press.

House-Midamba, B (1990) 'The United Nations Decade: Political Empowerment or Increased Marginalisation for Kenyan Women?' in *Africa Today* 1st Quarter, 1990, pp. 37–47.

Howard-Borjas, P (1989) *La Mujer Hondureña: Problemas para su Incorporación al Proceso de Desarollo Nacional via Proyectos*, Tegucigalpa, PNUD/FNUAP.

_____ (1990) *Empleo y Pobreza Rurales en Honduras, con Enfoque Especial en la Mujer Documento de Trabajo*, Tegucigalpa, SECPLAN/FNUAP.

_____ (1989) *Evolución de la Participación Feminina y la Discriminación en la Fuerza de Trabajo Hondureña: Implicaciones para políticas y Programas de Empleo Documento de Trabajo*, Tegucigalpa, SECPLAN.

Hunt, D (1989) *Theories of Economic Development: An Analysis of Competing Paradigms*, London, Harvester Wheatsheaf.

IHDER (1986) *Memoria del Seminario Taller sobre "Participación y Organisación de la Mujer Campesina"*, Tegucigalpa, IHDER.

Inter-American Foundation (1994) *Grassroots Development* 18:2

Inter-Hemispheric Education Resource Center (1988) *Private Organisations with US Connections: Honduras*, Albuquerque, IHERC.

International Labour Office (1986) *Economically Active Population Estimates, 1950-1980; Projections 1985-2025*, Geneva, ILO.

Jackins, H (1983) *The Reclaiming of Power*, Seattle, Rational Island Publishers.

Jackson, C (1994) 'Rescuing Gender from the Poverty Trap'. Paper presented to the conference on 'Gender Research and Development: Looking Forward to Beijing', University of East Anglia.

Jacobs, B D (1992) *Fractured Cities: Capitalism, Community and Empowerment*, London, Routledge.

Jesani, A (1990) 'Limits of Empowerment: Women in Rural Health Care' in *Economic and Political Weekly* 19.5.90, pp. 1098–1103.

Johnson, H (1992) 'Women's Empowerment and Public Action: Experiences from Latin America' in Wuyts et al (eds.) (1992) pp. 147–174.

Kabeer, N (1994a) *Reversed Realities: Gender Hierarchies in Development Thought*, London, Verso.

_____ (1994b) 'Empowerment from Below: Learning from the Grassroots' in Kabeer (1994a), pp. 223–263.

Kardam, N (1991) *Bringing Women In: Women's Issues in International Development Programmes*, Boulder, Lynne Rienner.

Kassam, Y (1989) 'Who benefits from Illiteracy? Literacy and Empowerment' in *Prospects* 19:4.

Kawas, M C and Zúñiga, M L (1991) *Profile of the Honduran Woman*, Tegucigalpa, CIDA.

Kearney, D and Keenan, E (1988) 'Empowerment: Does anyone know what it means?' *Lynx* 34, 3–5.

Keller, B and Mbewe, D C (1991) 'Policy and Planning for the Empowerment of Zambia's Women Farmers' in *Canadian Journal of Development Studies* 12:1, 75–88.

Kelly, L (1992) 'The Contradictions of Power for Women': Paper given to the NFHA Women and Housing Conference, April. Mimeo.

Khan, N and Stewart, E (1994) 'Institution Building and Development in Three Women's Organisations: Participation, Ownership and Autonomy' in *The Journal of Social Studies* 63, pp. 53–82.

Kowalski, K M (1989) 'The Components of Empowerment from the Perspective of Successful Leaders in Business and Education' Unpublished PhD thesis, University of Pittsburgh.

Kroeker, C J (1993) 'Empowerment Programs for the Severely Disadvantaged: Lessons from a Process of Evaluation of a Nicaraguan Agricultural Co-operative'. Unpublished PhD thesis, Claremont Graduate School, California.

Kuhn, J (1990) *La Mujer Hondureña Marginada: un Acercamiento a su Problemática*, Tegucigalpa, SNV.

La Tribuna, Tegucigalpa.

Langness, L L and Frank, G (1981) *Lives: An Anthropological Approach to Biography*, Novato, Ca., Chandler and Sharp.

Lapper, R and Painter, J (1985) *Honduras: State for Sale*, London, Latin America Bureau.

Lather, P (1991) *Getting Smart: Feminist Research and Pedagogy with/in the postmodern*, London, Routledge.

Lavrin, A (1993) 'Women in Latin America: Current Research Trends' in Acosta-Belén, E and Bose, C E (eds.) (1993) *Researching Women in Latin America and the Caribbean*, Boulder, Westview Press.

Lazzari, M M (1990) 'Empowerment, Gender Content and Field Education'. Unpublished PhD thesis, Univerity of Denver.

Lee, J A B (1991) 'Empowerment through Mutual Aid Groups' in *Groupwork* 4:1, pp. 5–21.

Long, N (1992) 'From Paradigm Lost to Paradigm Regained: The case for an Actor-Oriented Sociology of Development' in Long and Long (1992), 16–46.

Long, N and Long, A (eds) (1992) *Battlefields of Knowledge: The Interlocking of Theory and Practice in Social Research and Development*, London, Routledge.

Longwe, S H (1991)'Gender Awareness: the Missing Element in the World Development Project' in Wallace,T (ed.) (1991).

Lopez de Mazier, A (1991) *La Mujer Hondureña Jefa de Hogar*, Tegucigalpa, FPNU.

_____ (1990) 'La Mujer Hondureña en Cifras', Tegucigalpa, mimeo.

Lorde, A (1984) *Sister Outsider*, Trumansburg, The Crossing Press.

Loutfi, M F (1987) 'Development with Women: Action, not Alibis' in *International Labour Review* 126:1.

Lugones, M C and Spelman, E (1983) 'Have we got a Theory for You! Feminist Theory, Cultural Imperialism and the Demand for the Woman's Voice' in *Women's Studies International Forum* 6, 573–581.

Lukes, S (1974) *Power: a Radical View*, London, Macmillan.

_____ (ed.) (1986) *Power*, Oxford, Blackwell.

Maguire, A (1992) 'Power: Now you see it, Now you Don't. A Woman's Guide to How Power Works' in McDowell, L and Pringle, R (1992).

Maradiaga Díaz, H (1990) *Analysis de la Situación de la Infancia y la Mujer en Honduras*, Tegucigalpa, UNICEF.

Marsden, D and Oakley, P (eds.) (1990) *Evaluating Social Development Projects*, Oxford, Oxfam.

May, R (1972) *Power and Innocence*, New York, W W Norton and Co.

McDowell, L (1993a) 'Space, Place and Gender Relations: Part 1. Feminist Empiricism and the Geography of Social Relations' in *Progress in Human Geography* 17:2, pp. 157–179.

_____ (1993b) 'Space, Place and Gender Relations: Part 2. Identity, Difference Feminist Geometries and Geographies' in *Progress in Human Geography* 17:3, pp. 305–318.

McDowell, L (1992) 'Doing Gender: Feminism, Feminists and Research Methods in Human Geography' in *Transactions of the Institute of British Geographers* 17, pp. 399–416.

McDowell, L and Pringle, R (1992) *Defining Women: Social Institutions and Gender Divisions*, Cambridge, Polity Press.

McKenzie, F (1992) 'Development from Within: the Struggle to Survive' in Taylor, D R F and McKenzie, F (eds.)(1992) *Development from Within: Survival in Rural Africa*, London, Routledge.

McWhirter, E H (1991) 'Empowerment in Counselling', *Journal of Counselling and Development* 69, 222–227.

Melendez, N (1992) 'Lineamientos Generales para el Trabajo de ANDAR con Mujeres: Una Propuesta para Orientar las Acciones', Tegucigalpa mimeo.

Mendoza, B (1989) 'Reflexiones en Torno a la Mujer y su Organizacion en Honduras', *Estudios Sociales Centroamericanos* 50.

Menike, K (1993) 'People's Empowerment from the People's Perspective' in *Development in Practice* 3:3, pp. 176–183.

Meyerding, J (1982) 'Reclaiming Nonviolence: Some Thoughts for Feminist Women who used to be Nonviolent, and Vice Versa' in McAllister, P (ed.) (1982) *Reweaving the Web of Life*, Philadelphia, New Society Publishers.

Meza Palma, M (1992) *Fecundidad, Educación y Servicios Básicos como Limitantes de Participación de la Mujer en el Desarollo Productivo*, Tegucigalpa, SECPLAN.

Mies, M (1983) 'Towards a Methodology for Feminist Research' in Bowles, G and Duelli Klein, R (1993) *Theories of Women's Studies*, London, Routledge.

de Miralda, R (1988) 'Organising Peasant Women in Honduras' in Levy, M F (1988) *Each in Her Own Way: Five Women Leaders of the Developing World*, Lynne Rienner.

Mitchell, G (1989) 'Empowerment and Opportunity' in *Social Work Today* 16.3.89.

Mohanty, C T (1991a) 'Under Western Eyes: Feminist Scolarship and Colonial Discourses' in Mohanty, Russo and Torres, (eds) (1991) pp. 51–80.

_____ (1991b) 'Cartographies of Struggles: Third World Women and the Politics of Feminism' in Mohanty, Russo and Torres,(eds) (1991), pp.1–50.

Mohanty, C T, Russo, A and Torres, L (eds) (1991) *Third World Women and the Politics of Feminism*, Bloomington, Indiana University Press.

Molyneux, M (1985) 'Mobilization without Emancipation: Women's Interests, State and Revolution in Nicaragua' in *Feminist Studies* 11: 2, pp 227–254.

Morley, L (1991) 'Towards a Pedagogy for Empowerment in Community and Youth Work Training' in *Youth and Policy* 35, December, pp. 14–19.

Moser, C (1989) 'Gender Planning in the Third World: Meeting Practical and Strategic Gender Needs' in *World Development* 17: 11, 1799–1825.

Moser, C (1993) *Gender Planning and Development: Theory, Practice and Training*, London, Routledge.

Mullender, A and Ward, D (1989) 'Gaining Strength Together' in *Social Work Today* 24.8.89.

Nichols, P (1991) *Social Survey Methods: A Fieldguide for Development Workers*, Oxford, Oxfam.

Nicholson, L J (ed.) (1990) *Feminism/Postmodernism*, London, Routledge.

Ngau, P M (1987) 'Tensions in empowerment: the experience of Harambee (self-help) movement, Kenya' in *Economic Development and Cultural Change* 35:3, 523–538.

Noé Pino, H, Thorpe, A and Sandoval Corea, R (1992) *El Sector Agricola y la Modernización en Honduras*, Tegucigalpa, CEDOH/POSCAE.

Oakley, P et al (1991) *Projects with People: the Practice of Participatary Rural Development*, Geneva, ILO.

Ong, A (1988) 'Colonialism and Modernity: Feminist Re-presentations of Women in Non-Western Societies' in *Inscriptions* 3:4, pp. 79–93.

Oxfam (1993) 'Gender and Development: Oxfam's policy for its Programme', Oxford, Oxfam.

Oyuela, I L de (1993) *Mujer, Familia y Sociedad*, Tegucigalpa, Editorial Guaymuras.

PAEM (1990a) *Conociéndome a mí Misma: Cuaderno de Temas*, Tegucigalpa, Programa Educativo para la Mujer.

PAEM (1990b) *Guía de la Animadora*, Tegucigalpa, PAEM.

Paniagua Cabrera, R M (1992) 'La Participación de la Mujer en Tareas y/o Proyectos Forestales' MA Thesis, Universidad Nacional Autónoma de Honduras.

Papanek, H (1990) 'To Each Less than she Needs, From Each More than she can Do' in Tinker (1990).

Parpart, J (1993) 'Who is the 'Other'?: A Postmodern Feminist Critique of Women and Development Theory' in *Development and Change* 24, pp. 439–464.

Parsons, R J (1991) 'Empowerment: Purpose and Practice Principle in Social Work' in *Social Work with Groups* 14:2, 7–21.

Patai, D (1991) 'US Academics and Third World Women: Is Ethical Research Possible' in Gluck, S B and Patai, D A (eds.) (1991) *Women's Words: The Feminist Practice of Oral History*, London, Routledge.

Pearce, J (1993) 'NGOs and Social Change: Agents or Facilitators?' in *Development in Practice* 3:3, pp. 222–227.

Pérez N and Ponce, F (1992) *Modulo de Mujer: Participación Económica de la Mujer Nota Técnica*, Tegucigalpa, SECPLAN.

Peters, T (1987) *Thriving on Chaos: Handbook for a Management Revolution*, London, Macmillan.

Pheterson, G (1990)'Alliances between Women: Overcoming Internalised Oppression and Internalised Domination' in Albrecht, A and Brewer, R M (eds) (1990).

Polsby, N W (1963) *Community Power and Political Theory*, New Haven and London, Yale University Press.

Posas, M (1989) *Modalidades del Proceso de Democratización en Honduras*, Tegucigalpa, Editorial Universitaria, Universidad Nacional Autónoma de Honduras.

Posgrado Centroamericano en Economía (1993) *El Impacto de las Políticas de Ajuste Estructural sobre el Medio Ambiente en Honduras*, Tegucigalpa, Universidad Nacional Autónoma de Honduras.

Posner, J L and McPherson, M (1982) 'Agriculture on the Steep Slopes of the Tropical Americas' in *World Development* 10:5, pp. 341–353.

Premchander, S (1994) 'Income Generating Programmes for Rural Women: Examining the Role of NGOs' in *Small Enterprise Development* 5:1, pp. 14–20.

Price, J (n.d.) 'Women's Development: Welfare Projects or Political Empowerment?' Amsterdam conference. Mimeo.

_____ (1992) 'Who Determines Need? A Case Study of a Women's Organisation in North India' in *IDS Bulletin* 23:1, pp. 50–57.

Price-Chalita, P (1994) 'Spatial Metaphor and the Politics of Empowerment: Mapping a Place for Feminism and Postmodernism in Geography?' in *Antipode* 26:3, pp. 236–254.

Radcliffe, S A (1994) '(Representing) Post-Colonial Women: Authority, Difference and Feminisms' in *Area* 26:1, pp. 25–32.

Radcliffe, S A and Westwood, S (eds) (1993) *Viva: Women and Popular Protest in Latin America*, London, Routledge.

Radtke, H L and Stam, H J (eds.)(1994) *Power/Gender: Social Relations in Theory and Practice*, London, Sage Publications.

Ramalho, T (1985) 'Towards a Feminst Pedagogy of Empowerment: the Male and Female voices in Critical Theory'. Unpublished PhD thesis, Ohio State University.

Ramamonjisoa, S (1993) 'Empowerment of Women and Democracy in Madagascar' in *Review of African Political Economy* 58, pp. 118–123.

Ramazanoglu, C (1992) 'Feminism and Liberation' in McDowell and Pringle (1992) pp. 276–292.

Rathgeber, E M (1990) 'WID, WAD,GAD: Trends in Research and Practice' in *The Journal of Developing Areas* 24, pp. 489–502.

Ribbens, J (1989) 'Interviewing — and "Unnatural Situation"?' in *Women's Studies International Forum* 12:6, pp. 579–592.

Riley, J (1990) *Getting the Most from your Data: A Handbook of Practical Ideas on how to Analyse Qualitative Data*, Bristol, Technical and Educational Services Ltd.

Rogers, B (1980) *The Domestication of Women: Discrimination in Developing Societies*, London, Kogan Page.

Rosales, S E (n.d.) 'Consideraciones Preliminares Sobre la Situación de la Mujer en Honduras', Tegucigalpa, mimeo.

Rose, G (1993) *Feminism and Geography: The Limits of Geographical Knowledge*, Cambridge, Polity Press.

Rose, K (1992) *Where Women are Leaders: The SEWA Movement in India*, London, Zed Books.

Rosenberg, M et al (1990) *Honduras: Pieza Clave de la Política de Estados Unidos en Centro América*, Tegucigalpa, CEDOH.

Rowlands, J M (1995) 'Empowerment examined: an exploration of the concept and practice of women's empowerment in Honduras', PhD Thesis, University of Durham.

Safilios-Rothschild, C (1983) 'Women and the Agrarian Reform in Honduras' in *Land Reform: Land Settlements and Co-operatives* 1:2, 15–24.

Samarasinghe, V (1993) 'Puppets on a String: Women's Wage Work and Empowerment among Female Tea Plantation Workers of Sri Lanka' in *Journal of Developing Areas* April, pp. 329–340.

Sawicki, J (1988) 'Feminism and the Power of Foucauldian Discourse' in Arac (1988).

Schenk-Sandbergen, L (1991) 'Empowerment of Women: Its Scope in a Bilateral Development Project' in *Economic and Political Weekly* 27.4.91.

Schor, N and Weed, E (eds.) (1994) *The Essential Difference*, Bloomington, Indiana University Press.

Schumacher, E F (1973) *Small is Beautiful: Economics as if People Mattered*, London, Abacus.

Schuurman, F J (ed) (1993) *Beyond the Impasse: New Directions in Development Theory*, London, Zed Press.

Schwerin, E W (1990) 'Mediation and Empowerment: Citizen Participation in Conflict Resolution'. Unpublished PhD thesis, University of Hawaii.

Scott, J (1985) *Weapons of the Weak: Everyday Forms of Peasant Resistance*, New Haven, Yale University Press.

Secretaria de Planificación, Coordinación y Presupuesto (1989a) *Politica Nacional para la Mujer*, Tegucigalpa, SECPLAN/PNUD/UNIFEM.

_____ (1989b) *Perfil Ambiental de Honduras*, Tegucigalpa, SECPLAN.

_____ (1990) *Censo Nacional de Población, 1988: Characterísticas Geograficas, Migratorias y Sociales de la Población*, Tegucigalpa, SECPLAN.

_____ (1992) *Reunión Técnica: Segmentación del Mercado Laboral Femenino*, Tegucigalpa, SECPLAN.

_____ (1993) *Encuesta Permanente de Hogares de Propositos Multiples* Tegucigalpa, SECPLAN.

Secretaria Ejecutiva del Gabinete Social (1992) *Plan de Acción Nacional Desarollo Humano, Infancia y Juventud 1992-2000*, Tegucigalpa, SECPLAN.

Sen, G and Grown, C (1988) *Development, Crises and Alternative Visions: Third World Women's Perspectives*, London, Earthscan.

Shaffir, W B and Stebbins, R A (eds.) (1991) *Experiencing Fieldwork: An Inside View of Qualitative Research*, London, Sage.

Sheridan, A (1980) *Michael Foucault: the Will to Truth*, London, Tavistock.

Shetty, S (1991) *Development Projects in Assessing Empowerment*, Occasional Paper Series No. 3, New Delhi, Society for Participatory Research in Asia.

Smart, B (1985) *Michael Foucault*, London, Tavistock.

Stanley, L and Wise, S (1993) *Breaking Out Again: Feminist Ontology and Epistemology*, London, Routledge.

Staples, L (1987) 'Powerful Ideas about Empowerment' mimeo.

Starhawk [aka Simos, M] (1987) *Truth or Dare: Encounters with Power, Authority and Mystery*, San Francisco, Harper and Row.

Staudt, K (1985) *Women, Foreign Assistance and Advocacy Administration*, New York, Praeger.

Stöhr, W B and Taylor, F (1981) *Development from Above or Below? The Dialectics of Regional Planning in Developing Countries*, Chichester, John Wiley and Sons.

Stonich, S C (1991a) 'The Promotion of Non-Traditional Agricultural Exports in Honduras: Issues of Equity, Environment and Natural Resource Management' in *Development and Change* 22 pp. 725–755.

_____ (1991b) 'Rural Families and Income from Migration: Honduran Households in the World Economy' in *Journal of Latin American Studies* 23:1, pp. 131–161.

Strauss, A L (1987) *Qualitative Analysis for Social Scientists*, Cambridge, Cambridge University Press.

Strauss, A L and Corbin, J (1990) *Basics of Qualitative Research: Grounded Theory Procedures and Techniques*, London, Sage.

Sultana, M (1988) 'Participation, Empowerment and Variation in Development Projects for Rural Bangladeshi Women'. Unpublished PhD thesis, Northeastern University.

Tábora, R (1992) *Democratizando la Vida: la Propuesta Metodologica de las Mijeres del PAEM*, Tegucigalpa, COMUNICA.

_____ (1993a) 'An Education Programme for Peasant Women in Honduras' in *Development in Practice* 3:1, pp. 48–51.

_____ (1993b) 'Rural Women and Communication in Honduras: Notes on Methodology' in *Adult Education and Development* 41, pp. 149–161.

Taliaferro, M B (1991) 'The Myth of Empowerment' in *Journal of Negro Education* 60:1, 1–2

Thomas, A (1992) 'Non-Governmental Organisations and the Limits to Empowerment' in Wuyts et al (eds.)(1992) pp. 117–146.

Tiempo, Tegucigalpa.

Tinker, I (1976) 'The Adverse Impact of Development on Women' in Tinker, I and Bramsen, M (1976) *Women and World Development*, Washington DC, Overseas Development Council.

———— (ed.) (1990) *Persistant Inequalities*, Oxford, Oxford University Press.

Todaro, M (1994) *Economic Development*, Fifth edition, New York, Longman.

Torre, D (1986) 'Empowerment: a Structured Conceptualization and Instrument Development'. Unpublished PhD thesis, Cornell University.

Townsend, J G (1995) with Arrevillaga, V, Bain, J, Caucino, S, Frenk, S F, Pacheco, S and Pérez, E *Women's Voices From the Rainforest*, London, Routledge.

———— (1993) 'Housewifization and Colonisation in the Colombian Rainforest' in Momsen, J and Kinnaird, V (eds.)(1993) *Different Places, Different Voices: Gender and Development in Africa, Asia and Latin America*, London, Routledge.

Toye, J (1987) *Dilemmas of Development*, Oxford, Blackwell.

UNDP (1993) *Human Development Report 1993*, New York, Oxford University Press.

UNICEF (1989) *The Invisible Adjustment: Poor Women and the Economic Crisis*, Santiago, UNICEF.

USAID (1982) *AID Policy Paper: Women in Development*, Washington DC USAID.

———— (1992a) *Portfolio Description (Summary)*, Tegucigalpa, Agriculture and Rural Development Office, USAID.

———— (1992b) *Gender Considerations in Development: Report to Congress*, Tegucigalpa, USAID.

Valdez, X (1992) 'The Women's Rural School: An Empowering Educational Experience' in Stromquist, N (1992) *Women and Education in Latin America: Knowledge, Power and Change*, Boulder, Lynne Rienner, pp. 277–302.

Vargas, V (1991) 'The Feminist Movement in Latin America: Between Hope and Disenchantment'. Paper presented to Workshop on 'Rethinking Emancipation: Concepts of Liberation', The Hague, 30.1.91–1.2.91.

———— (1990) 'The Women's Movement in Peru: Streams, Spaces and Knots', The Hague, Institute of Social Studies, mimeo.

Vega-Carballo, J L (1989) 'Parties, Political Development and Social Conflict in Honduras and Costa Rica: a Comparative Analysis' in Flora, J L and Torres-Piras, E (eds.) (1989) *Sociology of "Developing Societies", Central America*, Basingstoke, Macmillan Education. pp. 92–111.

Villarreal, Magdalena (1992) 'The Poverty of Practice: Power, Gender and Intervention from an Actor-Oriented Perspective' in Long, N and Long, A (1992).

Villarreal, Marcela (1992a) *Lineamientos Generales para Incorporar Acciones Dirigidas a la Mujer*, Tegucigalpa, SECPLAN.

_____ (1992b) *Orientaciones para Abordar la Problemática de la Mujer en Honduras*, Bases para la Acción Tegucigalpa, SECPLAN.

Walby, S (1990) *Theorizing Patriarchy*, Oxford, Blackwell.

Walker, I (1992) 'El Trasfondo Político-Económico del Fomento de las Exportaciones No Tradicionales en América Central: el Ajuste Estructural y sus Efectos Sociales' in Mendizábal, A B and Jürgen Weller, P (1992) *Exportaciones Agricolas No Tradicionales: Promesa o Espejismo?*, Panama, CADESCA-PREALC (OIT).

Wallace, T with March, C (eds.) (1991) *Changing Perceptions: Writings on Gender and Development*, Oxford, Oxfam.

Ward, D and Mullender, A (1991) 'Empowerment and Oppression: An indissoluble pairing' in *Critical Social Policy* 11:2, 21–30.

Wartenberg, T E (1988) 'The Concept of Power in Feminist Theory' in *Praxis International* 8, October, pp. 301-316.

Washington Office on Latin America (1984) *Latin America: Honduras: A Democracy in Demise*, Washington DC WOLA.

Wasserstrom, R (1985) *Grassroots Development in Latin America and the Caribbean: Oral Histories of Social Change*, New York, Praeger.

Watts, M (1991) 'Entitlements or Empowerment? Famine and Starvation in Africa' in *Review of African Political Economy* 51, pp. 9–26.

Weber, M (1947) *The Theory of Economic and Social Organisation*, London, Routledge and Kegan Paul.

Werner, D (1989) *Donde no hay Doctor*, London, Macmillan. Copyrght The Hesperian Foundation, Box 1692, Palo Alto, California.

West, R C and Augelli, J P (1966) *Middle America: Its Lands and Peoples*, Englewood Cliffs, New Jersey, Prentice-Hall.

White, S C (1992) *Arguing with the Crocodile: Gender and Class in Bangladesh*, London, Zed Press.

Wieringa, S (1994) 'Women's Interests and Empowerment: Gender Planning Reconsidered' in *Development and Change* 25, 849–878.

Williams, S with Seed, J and Mwau, A (1995) *The Oxfam Gender Training Manual*, Oxford, Oxfam.

Wilson, F (1985) 'Women and Agricultural Change in Latin America: Some Concepts Guiding research' in *World Development* 13:9, pp. 1017–1035.

Wolfinger, R E (1971) 'Nondecisions and the study of Local Politics', *American Political Science Review* 65: 4, 1063–1080.

Wolin, S S (1988) 'On the Thoery and Practice of Power' in Arac (1988), pp. 179–201.

Womankind Worldwide (1994) 'Adopting and Managing a Project', draft internal document.

World Bank (1980) *World Development Report 1980*, Oxford, Oxford University Press.

_____ (1994) *World Development Report 1994*, Oxford, Oxford University Press.

Wuyts, M, Mackintosh, M and Hewitt, T (eds.)(1992) *Development Policy and Public Action*, Oxford, Oxford University Press.

Young, G, Samarasinghe, V and Kusterer, K (eds)(1993) *Women at the Center: Development Issues and Practices for the 1990s*, Hartford, Kumarian Press.

Young, K (1988a) *Women and Economic Development: Local, Regional and National Planning Strategies*, Oxford, Berg.

_____ (1988b) 'Gender and Development: a Relational Approach', Brighton, Institute of Development Studies, mimeo.

Young, K (1993) *Planning Development with Women: Making a World of Difference*, London, Macmillan.

Yudelman, S W (1987) 'The Integration of Women into Development Projects: Observations on the NGO Experience in General and in Latin America in Particular' in *World Development* 15, Supplement. pp. 179–187.

Yuval-Davies, N (1994) 'Women, Ethnicity and Empowerment' in *Feminism and Psychology* 4:1 pp 179–197.

Zacharakis-Jutz, J (1988) 'Post-Freirean Adult Education: a Question of Empowerment and Power' in *Adult Education Quarterly* 39:1, pp. 41–47.

Zimmerman, M A (1990) 'Toward a Theory of Learned Hopefulness: A Structural Model Analysis of Participation and Empowerment' in *Journal of Research in Personality* 24:1, pp. 71–86.

Zuñiga, M and Hernández, O(1989) 'Poor Women and the Economc Crisis: the Case of Honduras' in UNICEF (1989).

Index

empowering communities
A Casebook from West Sudan

Peter Strachan with Chris Peters

This casebook examines the way in which a participative approach to development can result in empowerment for communities.

Empowering Communities is an account of the Kebkabiya project in the west of Sudan. The project began as an attempt to improve food security in the wake of a major famine, but over the years, many other initiatives have been introduced. Oxfam initially managed all the project activities; but responsibility for the project has been largely handed over to a community-based organisation. The account of the increasing involvement of the community, and the creation of democratic structures for managing the project, provides valuable insights into the way in which a participative approach to development can result in empowerment for communities. One particularly interesting aspect of the work in Kebkabiya is how the problem of women's impoverishment and disempowerment within a strongly patriarchal society was addressed.

There were many setbacks and problems to be faced. The general insecurity resulting from a long-running war was an ever-present threat to project activities. The economy of the country was unstable, and rapid inflation threatened the viability of savings and credit schemes. The concept of democratic representation was not part of the traditional culture. Peter Strachan considers these problems, and how they were tackled, and reports the views of the people involved, to give the reader a real sense of development in action.

Peter Strachan worked for Oxfam in Sudan for three years, and was particularly concerned with the development of the Kebkabiya project. Chris Peters is a writer and researcher on development issues, and is the author of the Oxfam Country Profile *Sudan: A Nation in the Balance* (1996).

April 1997   0 85598 358 2   paperback / 96pp illustrated / £7.95 $12.95

United Kingdom and Ireland

Capacity-Building

An Approach to People-Centred Development   *Deborah Eade*

new

The prime purpose of Oxfam and similar development agencies is to assist poor men and women in changing their situation and exercising their right to participate in the development of their societies. However, aid agencies that ignore people's *existing* strengths may create dependency, and so make people more vulnerable than before.

This book examines the concept of capacity-building and why it is such an integral part of development theory. It considers specific and practical ways in which NGOs can contribute to enabling people to build on the capacities they already possess, whilst avoiding undermining such capacities.

Capacity Building reviews the types of social organisation with which NGOs might consider working, and the provision of training in a variety of skills and activities, for the people involved and for their organisation. The particular importance of using a capacity- building approach in emergency situations, and of the dynamic and long-term nature of the process, is also emphasised.

Deborah Eade is a writer and researcher on development theory and practice, with several years of experience as an Oxfam Deputy Regional Representative in Central America. She is currently editor of the international quarterly *Development in Practice* and is a regular consultant for major international agencies. She is co-author of *The Oxfam Handbook of Development and Relief* (1995).

An Oxfam Development Guideline
July 1997   0 85598 366 3   paperback / 160pp / £8.95 $14.95

United Kingdom and Ireland

Oxfam (UK and Ireland) publishes a wide range of books, manuals and resource materials for specialist, academic and general readers, and for schools.
For free catalogues, please contact:
Oxfam Publishing
274 Banbury Road
Oxford
OX2 7DZ, UK.
fax: +44 (0) 1865 313925
e-mail: publish@oxfam.org.uk

We welcome readers' comments on any aspects of Oxfam publications. Please write to the editorial team at:
Oxfam Publications
274 Banbury Road
Oxford
OX2 7DZ, UK.